I've known Noel since he was just a teenager. Even then he was quoting, "The only thing necessary for the triumph of evil is for good men to do nothing." He has lived his life that way and it has propelled him to this, writing a book and creating a company dedicated to destroying the evil of human trafficking. I know of no other person as passionate on this issue than Noel Thomas and this book demonstrates that fact.

—*John Terech*
COO of ECO: A Covenant Order of Evangelical Presbyterians

Dark Watch has mapped 32,000 brothels run by 200 crime organizations and is bringing to market a scalable solution that has huge potential to help the banks, hotels, social media, and rideshare companies that are being used by these crime networks to turn the tide in the fight against trafficking.

—*Wes Lyons*
General Partner, Eagle Venture Fund

Dark Traffic is both a key tool and a wake-up call in the fight against trafficking. Noel Thomas provides readers with vital knowledge about the networks and perpetrators of these crimes, who use technology to further their schemes against the vulnerable and innocent. Your family, friends, and community members deserve protection from this industry, and reading and sharing the helpful information in this book is a great first step.

—*Elizabeth Good*
Author of *Speak the Unspeakable* and *Groomed*,
Founder/CEO of The Foundation United

DARK
TRAFFIC

NOEL THOMAS
WITH ROB SUGGS

DARK TRAFFIC

THE DANGEROUS INTERSECTION OF TECHNOLOGY, CRIME, MONEY, SEX, AND HUMANITY

WHITAKER
HOUSE

DARK TRAFFIC
The Dangerous Intersection of Technology, Crime, Money, Sex, and Humanity

Noel Thomas
https://darkwatch.io

Rob Suggs
www.robsuggs.com
robsuggs@gmail.com

ISBN: 979-8-88769-231-9
eBook ISBN: 979-8-88769-232-6
Printed in the United States of America
© 2024 by Noel Thomas

Whitaker House
1030 Hunt Valley Circle
New Kensington, PA 15068
www.whitakerhouse.com

Library of Congress Control Number: 2024937248

1 2 3 4 5 6 7 8 9 10 ⊔⊔ 31 30 29 28 27 26 25 24

CONTENTS

DEDICATION

This book is dedicated to the countless victims and survivors of trafficking. Your voice matters.

ACKNOWLEDGEMENTS

This book, and the ministry it describes, owe especially deep gratitude to the following people:

My wife

Mom and Dad

My sister and brother-in-law

My mother-in-law, father-in-law, and sister-in-law

John Terech

Jack Haye

Abby Taylor

Samuel Curet

Ben Leichtliner

Terry Brent

Greg Smith

Brandon Kelley

Rhonda Graff

Jan Edwards

Kathleen Winn

Tammy Toney-Butler

Kristin Vaughn

Rob Suggs

Chip MacGregor

John Caulfield

Lynda Lanier

PROLOGUE

Every now and then, Angela remembers her previous life. She used to be someone else—an ordinary girl, a free girl.

Not exactly a perfect girl. Maybe not even a happy one, at least there at the end. Angela fought with her parents. She ran around with friends they did not like—friends who would smoke cigarettes and listen to Nirvana till two in the morning. The kind that would commit petty theft because they enjoyed the rush of kleptomania.

Angela has come to realize that may be why she ran around with them in the first place. During those couple of rough years of being a teenager, rebelling just to rebel was the escape she needed from ordinary suburbia. No different from most of the kids she knew.

But then came that terrible night and that awful, screaming argument. Her mom had gone through her things without asking and found the drugs. Angela never considered marijuana a drug; in her eyes, it was more of a tool to take the edge off. Her mom thought otherwise.

Angela ran away that night, not pausing to consider where she would go or how she would survive.

She hopped on a bus, walked around town aimlessly for a few hours, and finally found some kids in a Waffle House. They reminded her of her friends at home. The kids listened to her story, then they took her to Rocco. (That's the only name she ever knew him by.) They said Rocco would know exactly what to do. He would have all the answers.

Rocco was a little older than the others, maybe in his mid-twenties, with a tight fade haircut, and he was eager to help. He offered Angela a place to stay and asked no questions. He listened as she vented all her frustration and anger concerning her parents. He nodded, hugged her, and held her when the tears began to flow. Then he gave her Jack Daniels and half a Xanax to soothe her and help her sleep.

As Angela faded off, emotionally spent, Rocco stayed right there with her, like a guardian angel.

The next day, he said all the things she longed to hear. Finally she had found her place in the world—a place that, despite being chaotically beautiful, she could call home.

Rocco did not call Angela's parents or the authorities. Instead, he counseled her to take some time, stick with him for a few days, enjoy some of his leftover cocaine, and sort things out. That sounded really good to Angela.

Between the highs from the coke, Rocco gave Angela pills that killed the pain. At first, the pills simply provided her with a way to shut out all the voices she heard in her head; they also numbed her painful memories, like that of the first time one of her friends had molested her. Eventually, though, the drugs became a destination in themselves, leading her to new journeys of higher highs, but also depressing lows.

Angela was unsure what Rocco did for a living, but he seemed to have money spilling out of his Gucci wallet. He drove a purple Dodge Challenger to his homes near Biscayne Bay and Miami.

One day he said, "Ang, I'm trying to help you, girl, but I'm not up for getting detained by the police and accused of kidnapping, ya know what I mean? They'll be looking for you. It's best we move around a little. We can stay under the radar while you figure things out." Rocco caressed her hair and her shoulder as he said these things. Angela thought he was so kind, so attentive. Within a couple of days, they were lovers. She wanted to be with him every moment.

Angela's recollection reality became seriously hampered by her new whirlwind lifestyle. Her drug usage became more severe as she tried fentanyl, which gave her a rush accompanied by a serene and heavenly feeling. Her pain melted into oblivion—but, at the same time, her concept of time took on a warped and fluid existence, like something from a Salvador Dalí painting. She had vague memories of sleeping with Rocco mixed with memories of sleeping with other guys, strangers. How did that even happen? She struggled to connect the dots of her behavior.

Before she had run away, Angela had been inexperienced sexually. She never would have chosen to be this sexually active, this reckless. But since running away, she had entered a hazy, dreamlike period during. She was obsessed with a new man—but she had to acknowledge that her daily life was one of prostitution. However, Angela did not believe she was a victim of human trafficking.

In moments of lucid sanity, between highs, Angela suffered from debilitating bouts of anxiety. She bit her nails down to the quick, leaving them bleeding. The cigarette in her hand looked weird somehow. She knew this was her hand but did not feel she was in her body. There were moments when she fantasized about going home—apologizing, reconciling, sleeping in her bed with too many pillows in her room that still had a few dolls and toys.

Prostitution had never been a life goal—that was certain. Human trafficking? The furthest thing from her mind.

She loathed the men who showed up, one after the other. She hated the kinds of things they demanded and being knocked bloody after a customer partook in a drug-fueled bender. More than anything else, she hated the lack of freedom. There were moments when Angela could have run—but where to? Her parents weren't going to give her the pills she craved. They certainly wouldn't put the needle in her arm. The police wouldn't. And her body *demanded* drugs 24/7, at any cost. If she wasn't high, she felt like she would die.

Tonight, looking around, Angela realizes she's sitting in that same Waffle House she had once entered, tears staining her face, when she was on the run, not much more than a naïve little girl. A few of the same kids are here with her. One or two have vanished. One overdosed.

Only now, Angela is one of the street girls helping to welcome a fresh runaway who reminds her so much of herself. Angela is trafficking someone else.

She smiles and tells this new kid, "We've got you, honey. And wait until you meet Rocco!"

In return for this service, Rocco will reward her. Maybe he'll toss her the leftovers of a bag of coke, or drop a few pills into her frail, shaking hand.

1

INTO THE SHADOWS

The gold SUV moved through the streets of Orlando, Florida—just one more piece in the daily traffic grind. But inside the vehicle, I felt a surge of adrenalin. This was my first raid on a human trafficking target.

I felt exhilaration and dread in equal portions. I knew quite well that lives were at stake. I didn't want to make some rookie blunder and ruin the team's months of planning and execution.

I calmed myself by closing my eyes and focusing on my breathing But all the while, I was cycling through different scenarios in my mind. Would the traffickers resist violently? Were they prepared for us? Or would we even find evidence?

I'd have been much more comfortable with a bass guitar in my hands, as when I'd toured with my rock group. What innocent times those were. But this moment was a choice I had made, and it was time to find out if I had the right stuff.

It had all started with a phone call from an old friend in law enforcement. He's the kind of guy who casually mentions breaking collarbones and ribs while wrestling bad guys to the ground. My life is pretty mundane in comparison.

"What's up?" I asked him, ready for one of his stories.

"Trafficking, of course," he said. "And I need your help."

"How so?"

"I'd rather not talk about it over the phone."

As it turned out, he'd learned about an old motel on the outskirts of town that was developing a shady reputation for trafficking and strung-out drug users. It looked to be one more front for a human trafficking operation.

"I'm in," I told him once I'd heard the details. How could you hear such things and simply turn away? I was willing to help however I could.

My friend had enlisted me because he knew I was good at uncovering information on the Internet, including the dark web. We spent the day following a trail of clues through advertising sites. Think furniture ads but replace the furniture with sex. This is where victims are bought and sold on online marketplaces, then come back to post "helpful" reviews, just like with Yelp or Google. The clues are there. You just have to know where to look.

We knew that any delay in action meant more destroyed lives. We expedited the arrangements for a raid, and my friend wanted me to be involved.

With the exception of me, everyone on the team was trained, experienced, and capable of tackling a trafficker fueled by steroids. Even so, the traffickers might be armed, prepared, and violent. And what about the victims? Would they even be willing to leave with us? This is always a complex question. Those running the operation will have some kind of hold on their victims. Most victims don't even recognize they are being trafficked; they believe they are willing sex workers.

The van slowed down, we parked, and light flooded in as the doors opened. I surveyed our surroundings. This was not exactly a neighborhood the city was proud of. We entered the hotel, and immediately I recoiled from the stench—a mix of perspiration, cheap perfume, and whatever composes fear. The team made its way to a cramped, dark, and dingy room scattered with heaps of clothing and the typical residue of human trafficking. I noticed an expensive pair of sneakers, a varsity jacket, and a billed cap.

A shriek from a shadowed corner of the room broke the silence. My eyes fell on the source of the noise: a girl huddled in the corner, cringing away from the threat we posed. Her eyes offered a dead gaze troubled by panic—a view of the world filtered through hopelessness, surrender, and sudden confusion.

My friend and I gently approached her with our palms up, exuding a calm, soothing demeanor. She flinched but didn't move away. "We're here to help," said my friend in his softest tone. "You're safe. We're here to help you and get you home." We gave her a few moments to adapt and come to terms with this idea. Eventually a hint of cautious relief overcame her.

To their victims, traffickers are omnipotent and godlike. They're also ruthless and willing to destroy anything or anyone that would threaten their business. It's hard for their devastated victims to believe in knights in shining armor—people capable of ushering these damaged victims beyond the clutches of their captors.

I understood that we needed to project confidence and authority. *No one will punish you for trusting us and accepting our help.*

We helped her gather her belongings, and we departed from her downtown prison—hopefully forever.

The operation was successful, but it really shook me. The girl's dead eyes and broken spirit stayed with me. Who was evil enough to build a business around inflicting that level of trauma on someone? And what could I do to stop them?

How many other victims were out there, imprisoned in hotel rooms?

UPDATING THE PICTURE

Our world is driven by consumerism. Any tangible thing can be bought or sold, and people are driven by attaining the purchasing power to acquire more and more coveted pleasures and possessions. It's a world in which drugs and weapons are easily procured. Cryptocurrency provides a covert way of managing capital, making it possible to stray from the financial grid and cover one's tracks.

The dark web offers a useful venue for illegal activities. On hidden websites, even human lives are for sale with untraceable currency—lives available to exploit and then discard. With these cloaks of secrecy, human trafficking can be very difficult to find and fight.

Yet many traffickers don't even bother with all that subterfuge. They use the mainstream Internet, local businesses, and busy thoroughfares. You might even find these activities being carried out within a block of your place of worship. After all, bringing in the "product" is important. Traffickers need to be where the people are—near schools, parks, and shopping malls. Like spiders, they weave webs of promises and enticements that lure naïve young people, then trap them in cycles of abuse and exploitation.

Still, the Internet provides the easiest way to find and attract the next round of victims, and cryptocurrency is quickly becoming the coin of the realm. Traffickers use false documents, encrypted communication, and bribe public officials who might be in the way.

According to some estimates, human trafficking generates more than $150 billion in illegal profits each year, and it finances a vast network of other criminal activities. With a market flourishing at this level, it's no wonder the criminals behind it are so careful to stay one step ahead of law enforcement.

Despite its growth, few people are aware of the scope of this problem. They tend to have a vague awareness of the term *trafficking*. But their vision of the issue is based on outdated ideas, maybe taken from something they saw on Netflix. Perhaps they think of the meth-addicted biker who sells young women to support his drug habit. That's old news. Now we're living in a world where the dark web, cryptocurrency, and large criminal organizations push mainstream trafficking operations, although family members trafficking their children to criminal organizations still remains one of the main categories of trafficking.

The response against trafficking is changing too. My organization, Dark Watch, is pioneering new strategies to usher in a new wave of counter-trafficking. We use advanced technology to get into the shadows and stay up to date on criminal activity—and we help the public do the same. We're geared toward training others and joining forces with agencies and organizations wherever possible, because there's strength in numbers, whether in data or partnerships. Collective action will begin to defeat traffickers.

Please understand that this probably won't be the one and only book you'll read on this issue. The problem will continue to wear new faces and try new approaches. Trafficking isn't a simple spot on the social fabric that can be quickly removed; it's a massive and deadly industry that crawls along a web woven by ISIS, Boko Haram, Asian organized crime, and Mexican drug cartels.

Crime organizations have continued to evolve, and the trafficking of humans and human organs is a path of lesser resistance than illegal drugs and weapons. This $150 billion industry pours funding into terrorism and drug cartels, fueling their violence globally. It continues to grow because it's one of the least risky crimes to prosecute.

If you're like most people, all of this is news to you. This book was written to bridge the information gap—and, consequently, the outrage gap. Lives are destroyed in large numbers, and we need to raise an army of awareness and determination to fight this enemy who is thriving in the shadows of our culture.

WHAT WE THINK WE KNOW

I'm at a party or in casual conversation somewhere, and I meet someone who asks me what I do. Once I tell them I fight trafficking, I expect a vague reaction, probably accompanied by ideas carried over from the last century. If I said I worked for the Drug Enforcement Agency or the Federal Bureau of Investigation, I wouldn't have to do much explaining. People tend not to know much about this field but don't realize it.

They assume trafficking happens mainly in Third World countries and is about smuggling. I get that. There's a fine line and a certain degree of overlap between trafficking and smuggling. Still, the two worlds are distinct.

My new friend at the party probably saw *Taken* (or one of its two sequels, since that movie turned out to be a box-office blockbuster). Liam Neeson, playing a father with a "unique set of skills," travels across the world to rescue his teenage daughter from a sex-trafficking ring. "That is an exciting movie," I tell my friend. "But just to be clear, I'm not much like Liam Neeson."

I'm thankful for the film *Taken* because it introduced many people to a horrifying problem, albeit packaged as a standard action movie. There was a spike in enrollment in anti-trafficking movements once that film hit the box office in 2008. Even today, it tends to come up in the first five minutes of casual conversation. But that film presents a mere snapshot of one sector of the true story. *Gladiator* doesn't give me a comprehensive picture of the Roman Empire; the James Bond series doesn't tell us everything we need to know about international espionage and *Taken* doesn't come close to capturing the full extent of the human-trafficking issue.

The anti-trafficking movement has gained ground in recent years, receiving increased visibility and energy from high-profile busts. For example, in 2021, the sting operation called Operation Ohio Knows arrested 161 people. In 2019, in my home state of Florida, a group of men was arrested for involvement in massage parlor prostitution. One of them was Robert Kraft, owner of the New England Patriots. He offered a plea of not guilty to misdemeanor charges, and then an appeals court ruled that the use of hidden cameras violated the men's constitutional rights. Thus, the charges were dropped—at least against the men. The positive angle was the publicity that came out of the incident due to the celebrity of an NFL team owner. People read the details, watched TV news accounts, and heard about the business connection to Chinese organized crime.

The power of celebrity in the United States sure is telling. It seems a show business angle is required in order to get people's attention. We needed a successful action movie to introduce the concept of human trafficking, and the spectacle of an NFL owner caught with his pants down to get people invested. And don't forget the sordid tale of Jeffrey Epstein and Ghislaine Maxwell, which still causes a huge swath of the population to cringe. By this time, people are beginning to get the picture that horrible things are going on just out of sight.

Epstein reaffirmed the frustrating lesson taught to us by Robert Kraft: the rich and famous enjoy a convenient shield from legal accountability. As *Taken* played in movie theaters across America, Epstein stood before a judge, convicted of child prostitution and solicitation of prostitution. A controversial plea deal amounted to a slap on the wrist, and Epstein and Maxwell went on their way, only to victimize more young women for more than a decade. Several high-profile individuals somehow dodged exposure to the public, and the whole saga slipped into the category of yesterday's news.

My new friend from the party? He's heard about the significant cases. He may not connect the events in *Taken* to the accounts from Florida or Ohio. Still, he begins to understand that sexual sickness is a rampaging contagion and that criminal networks, large and small, are finding ways to profit from it. He wants to do something, to light a candle rather than curse the darkness. But where are such candles found? And how are they lit?

He doesn't know what he can do to help.

Maybe he will tell a friend about his feelings the next day at work. "Yeah, it's awful stuff. But you might as well stop the rain from falling. You're one guy; the people who run this racket are serious gangsters. Everybody just needs to be careful and protect their daughters. Besides—nobody gets justice these days. Not if they have a good lawyer. The world's not fair."

This book is written first to provide information. The public desperately needs a clear and accurate understanding of our problem, since it threatens the people we love. Second, I hope this book makes people angry, because anger focused in the right direction is righteous. We ought to be angry when people's lives are being destroyed.

Third, I want to dispel the myth that one person can't do very much. Because I'm one person, and I was overwhelmed, too, when I came to understand what was happening in my world. Yet I've come to understand that mass movements are made up of lots of "one persons" who come together to become one massive force for good.

Let me tell you more about the complicated web of trafficking, about Dark Watch and our efforts to stop trafficking, along with some informational stories.

2

FOLLOW THE MONEY

Dark Watch is data driven. Much like Liam Neeson, we have a unique set of skills, though the resemblance abruptly ends there. Our skills involve numbers and information. The Hollywood film about our work wouldn't be nearly as exciting, but I hope we'd disrupt a lot more networks than Liam's character did.

We analyze digital footprints and train people on the front lines according to what we're discovering. Digital intelligence is our primary weapon, and it helps us act rather than react. We find trends and make predictions, which enables us to track the sophisticated criminal organizations that are the biggest threats. We also provide this data, along with training and resources, to others in the fight to stop trafficking. Through our Dark Watch platform, we bring together a vast network of entities who come together in this fight.

Dark Watch data, as we call it, is designed with two goals in mind: to disrupt human trafficking networks and to stop these predators from abusing the financial system.

I've mentioned that criminals see trafficking as a low-risk endeavor. Through it, they can raise significant funding with less exposure than other ventures. However, we're gradually increasing their risks as we use our technical expertise to fill in the gaps of traditional law enforcement, which simply hasn't had the expertise and the technology to home in on traffickers.

The standard approach of the justice system has been victim-centric cases, which have mostly been unreliable. Traumatized victims are painfully questioned in detail and then asked to appear in court only to relive their trauma through additional questioning. In such cases, the victim is largely the only tangible evidence to work from.

There are limits to the effectiveness of this approach. For example, I recall a case involving a young woman who'd been ensnared by a violent trafficker who was part of a fentanyl distribution network. We worked with law enforcement agencies and the woman's parents, providing intel on her location, to make a meeting possible that we hoped would sever her connection to those exploiting her. We arranged to get her together with her dad. It wasn't easy; multiple law enforcement agencies were involved, and all the logistics had to be tight and well-coordinated. A second woman, also being trafficked, was to bring the young lady in a van to meet us. Working with her added another layer of complexity.

I'll never forget seeing the young lady emerge from the van and sprint into her father's arms. "It's so good to see you! I've missed you so much," she said repeatedly through her tears.

He was equally overwhelmed. "I've missed you too, sweetheart. Let's get you home—"

"I can't!" she interjected. "I don't have my fentanyl. I must be able to get it."

"No, honey. Come on, let's leave that behind."

He was firm. With doubt in her eyes, she accompanied him. But two hours later, the withdrawal pangs overwhelmed her. She returned to the trafficker, who was her only source for the drug.

We were all heartsick, and we knew the feeling too well. It never becomes easier to watch someone choose bondage to narcotics over freedom and love; it's a feeling of despair. No wonder criminals use fentanyl and other drugs to trap their victims. The controlling power of illegal drugs is almost impossible to overcome; these substances can enslave those who use them.

Even if we can free someone and get them into court as a witness, an effective lawyer can pick their stories apart. The victims may still be under the influence of narcotics, forced to function in a world where truth and fantasy intertwine. On the witness stand, their testimony can be deemed not credible, and their captors walk free.

Nor is it pleasant to force someone who's been traumatized to keep reliving these experiences through depositions and legal questioning. And even then, victims can die before a case ever comes to trial.

The sad truth is that trafficking is severely damaging, but serving as the focal point of law enforcement continues the agony.

At Dark Watch, we've seen this problem over and over as a well-meaning justice system attempts to seize on help from their only actual witnesses: those who have been abused and exploited and who need love, gentle therapy, and as much distance as possible from a painful past. We've concentrated on alternatives that spare much of that pain and attack the problem from entirely different angles.

HIT THEM WHERE IT HURTS

Dark Watch provides prosecutors with data evidence that can create charges for financial crimes. RICO (the Racketeer Influenced and Corrupt Actions Act) is one avenue we can take. Another is tax evasion. Thus, we're adjusting the target and hitting the supply-and-demand sides of organized crime networks. I call it "cutting off the Hydra's heads." The Hydra was a many-headed serpent in Greek mythology. We recognize that this kind of crime has many faces, and some are more vulnerable than others.

What we care about ultimately is the victim, the life destroyed. But for the criminal, it's all about the money. That's where we come after the perpetrators. We hit them where it hurts the most and, in so doing, take the harmful glare off the survivors, who have suffered enough. In the courtroom, money testifies clearly and powerfully. Lawyers can't call it a liar, attack it for memory lapses, or ruin its credibility.

We weren't the first to rely on this strategy. In the 1980s, Rudy Giuliani, as US attorney for the Southern District of New York, used RICO to prosecute the so-called "Five Families" of New York organized crime. Racketeering is often associated with other forms of crime, and it leaves paper trails that can be useful in apprehending criminals who would be difficult to stop otherwise.

In the wake of the Epstein fallout, the banking industry has begun to pay more attention to our work. Banks are required by law to file reports alerting federal authorities to any suspicious activities. Deutsche Bank was fined $150 million for failing to flag hundreds of suspicious transactions involving Epstein's account.[1]

If you've followed the news, you know that money laundering has grown into a massive problem. This is the process of covering the tracks of money that has been raised illegally. Billions of dollars of drug money, for example, flow through businesses set up simply to "launder," or wash away, the stain of illegality. The banking industry has figured out that we need better weapons against money laundering. We at Dark Watch aid banks in tackling money

---

1. Press Release, "Superintendent Lacewell Announces DFS Imposes $150 Million Penalty on Deutsche Bank in Connection with Bank's Relationship with Jeffrey Epstein and Correspondent Relationships with Danske Estonia And FBME Bank," New York State Department of Financial Services, July 7, 2020, https://www.dfs.ny.gov/reports_and_publications/press_releases/pr202007071.

laundering because, wherever trafficking is involved, money laundering will also be involved.

Dark Watch provided a large regional bank in Texas with data on individuals we suspected of trafficking in that area. The bank ran our data against its accounts and found 177 matches. That was impressive. Then, they randomly selected one—who happened to be a registered massage therapist—and they investigated. It turned out that the therapist was depositing an estimated $280,000 per month from unknown sources. That works out to $3.3 million per year. These figures would equate to quite a few massages in a typical parlor, identified or not.

Consider this: the setting of this massage parlor was a suburban shopping center. It could have been around the corner from your home.

Some of the strongest reactions I receive from the audiences I speak to about trafficking come from sharing that piece of information. Money laundering isn't only a crime committed in distant countries; it has moved into our neighborhoods, hiding in plain sight. At the time of this writing, three women were convicted of money laundering associated with prostitution rings within massage parlors in Williamsburg and Virginia Beach, Virginia[2]—nice communities indeed. Victims of trafficking can certainly come from impoverished countries, but they can also be college-age American students baited by get-rich-quick schemes.

But where does the money come from? Exactly where most people would try to raise funds: in the world's most prosperous nations, including the United States.

---

2. Press Release, "Third Defendant in Williamsburg and Virginia Beach Money Laundering and Prostitution Massage Parlor Scheme Sentenced," United States Attorney's Office Eastern District of Virginia, December 1, 2023, https://www.justice.gov/usao-edva/pr/third-defendant-williamsburg-and-virginia-beach-money-laundering-and-prostitution.

THE PROBLEM HITS HOME

As I travel the country to speak to audiences, I get a lot of mileage from our community human trafficking map application. A local map is worth one thousand words. I simply pull up my current whereabouts—the epicenter for the audience—and they immediately understand that Dark Watch has a point. Suddenly, trafficking is no longer the stuff of TV crime shows. The app is showing them their own homes, shops, and places of worship.

The app uses green dots to show suspected active massage brothels and red dots to mark parlors that may have recently closed. I explain that red doesn't necessarily mean authorities have caught someone there or driven them from the business. These predators move around a lot, closing shop in one place and reopening elsewhere with a new name and the same network. They understand that moving targets are hard to hit.

As my audience connects the dots, there's an audible gasp. "That's near our grocery store! That's near our kids' school!"

One day, I was showing a friend a map of the city where we live. He asked me to zoom in on his church and its neighborhood. Seven suspected massage brothels were within close range. He just stared as the reality of what I'd told him sunk in. Then he looked at me and said, "I want you to come speak at our church. We need to get involved."

This is the launch point for people: the GPS factor—realizing it isn't someone else's problem. And what can one person do? Maybe a little more if it's my neighborhood we're talking about.

My brother-in-law knew how persuasive those maps could be. He asked me for a red-and-green-dotted screenshot of his hometown. I sent him one. I heard nothing back from him, but the next time the whole family gathered for my niece's baptism, he brought up the screenshot at the dinner table. Everyone there got into the discussion of where those dots were. They knew me well and had heard a lot about my work, but they were as shocked as anyone else to learn what was happening around them.

At a money laundering conference (which is every bit as delightful as it sounds), a woman walked up to me during a break and asked me to show her "the little map thing." She was half-joking, half-skeptical of the accuracy of our data. She assured me she lived in "the safest part of Massachusetts." And besides, weren't we "exaggerating a bit?"

I found her city on my phone app and began to zoom in. I let her see the map, which was dotted with enough red and green to look like the holiday season had come. She took a closer look, then her smile faded away. "I've been to this place," she said, pointing. "I was looking for a legitimate massage, and the 'therapist' hurt my wrist. I just figured it was a bad session or a bad masseur and didn't go back. I would never have thought …"

I smiled at her and said, "You're part of the problem, ma'am—you're supporting these places." Of course, she knew I was joking. We laughed, and then she was eager to receive suggestions about how she could become involved in the fight.

FIGHTING THE OCTOPUS

The Houston, Texas, chapter of Crime Stoppers also liked the map approach. Its leaders wanted to know if we could integrate our data with reported fentanyl overdoses, maybe by adding another color of dot.

Fentanyl is the hot opioid for pain management and, of course, abuse. It's fifty to one hundred times more potent than morphine, and in 2021, it caused close to 71,000 deaths.[3] So, there's a great deal of attention being given to fentanyl, along with other narcotics, in the opioid crisis.

3. "Drug Overdose Death Rates," National Institute on Drug Abuse, National Institutes of Health, https://nida.nih.gov/research-topics/trends-statistics/overdose-death-rates#:~:text=.

Technology has limitless possibilities. Our team is taking a closer look at the intersection of fentanyl overdoses with suspected trafficking. It could be one more way to smoke out criminals in hiding. It's also an example of how specialized organizations can help one another. Crime Stoppers was also interested in studying the proximity of trafficking to school zones, where children present a window of vulnerability as they walk home from school. It's a terrifying thought.

Our work with open-information data sets is still in its early days. A lot needs to be accomplished but realizing that we're tackling a rare issue with bipartisan political support is encouraging. How many public problems can you name where leaders of both parties are in complete agreement? The Trump and Biden administrations have both enacted national action plans to combat human trafficking. The US Department of the Treasury listed stopping human trafficking as one of its top eight priorities. Local political candidates also call us as they put together their plans to fight local crime. However, the significant change is that individuals are contacting us to find out how and where they can help.

All crime is offensive and unpleasant to think about, but the reality of trafficking hits us in the gut. We don't want it to exist anywhere, but the suggestion of its existence energizes us locally. We must act.

And the added angle of organized crime's involvement ups the ante. Human trafficking, when seen clearly, is a cancer on our world, an assault on decency.

Then we think of our children. There are things we do spiritually, educationally, and financially to care for our children's future, but this is about the here and now.

This is an "everything everywhere all at once" problem. Trafficking funds the precursors to fentanyl, the newest crisis. This crime impacts banks. Commercial real estate values take a hit as human trafficking occurs in strip malls in most towns. National security is endangered, as international terrorists, too, see the financial opportunities they can exploit. The next suicide bomber you hear about on the news could have been financed at least partially by human trafficking.

In other words, this is an octopus with countless deadly tentacles, and each one reaches into some safe and secure segment of daily life.

Criminals are attracted to trafficking because they perceive it as a low-risk venture. Trafficking has been happening out of the public eye, in the shadows, and people haven't seemed to care. Law enforcement doesn't seem to have the resources, and federal authorities have other things on their plate. But we can change that—and we already are.

As you hold this book, you're already becoming part of the solution. Can you feel it? The beginning of awareness is the beginning of caring and, ultimately, action.

So how? What? These pages will lay out the answers in practical ways. We'll show you how to spot signs of trafficking. Chapter eight, for example, will share twenty-five everyday industries affected by trafficking. Some will be part of your ordinary experience. One may be your daily workplace.

It's time for all of us to open our eyes.

3

THE ROAD LESS TAKEN

I pursue a unique line of work, but the path I took to get there is even more unusual. I was playing in a rock band on a successful European tour.

Most guys just out of college would have loved such an opportunity—a bucket-list-quality thrill. But for a kid who was once the target of playground bullies, it was more meaningful still.

I'd gotten off to a rough start in the traditional school system. Early on, my parents decided to pull me out of the system and homeschool me. Not fitting in was the beginning of my journey toward a countercultural mindset. I was an individual, a self-starter, a curious innovator with no interest in following the crowd. Therefore, nontraditional education was right for me.

I loved researching, collecting information, and educating myself in areas where public school would never have taken me. I could learn skateboarding instead of taking a PE class and participate in extreme sports instead of track and field. I played video games geared to teach more effectively than a teacher at a blackboard. Science was fishing in the ocean; history was visiting a national museum. And all of it was to my liking. I moved at my own speed and began to accelerate.

By the time I'd earned my high school diploma, I'd also completed two years of college work, and it wasn't long before I graduated from Florida Atlantic University with a degree in small business entrepreneurship. My true passion was punk rock and heavy metal; there I found my crowd, my tribe. A tight-knit group of us rallied around this common musical interest, and I finally experienced genuine community.

We were misfits and outcasts, ignored by the cool kids but perfectly comfortable in our little society with our own rules. We showed up without fail to support local bands, and then we'd hang out in the Taco Bell parking lot, laughing and talking until the early morning hours.

I became more of a fan of the metal scene and wanted to perform. I spent time in Arms Embrace, a Christian death metal band, as their screaming vocalist. In 2005, a nucleus from Arms Embrace started Constella Chapters. I played the keytar (keyboard synthesizer worn around the neck with a strap). Constella Chapters was a lighter electro-pop-sounding band. We weren't a household name in the United States, but we did catch fire in Europe.

These two bands shared musicians but little else—they were of different genres and attracted different audiences. But I enjoyed expressing both the lighter and heavier sides of my personality.

In 2007, Constella Chapters traveled to Europe for a tour, putting my small business entrepreneurship plans on hold. I was enthusiastic about traveling and proceeding to rock in a Christian way.

It was during our tour that a particular booklet fell into my hands. Be careful what you read—it might send your life careening down a whole different path.

THE TELLTALE BOOKLET

Part of the fun of a tour is that you get to perform in all kinds of venues. In the concert world, superstars only play in stadiums and enormous halls. But the rest of us—the everyday musicians—play outdoors and indoors, in theaters and churches, at taverns and street festivals, anywhere we can find an audience. Our group played at pubs, large gatherings, and churches here and there. The audiences were appreciative.

Someone handed me a pamphlet during a prayer night in Birmingham, England. I hardly noticed; people pass out leaflets and fliers all the time. We were in a room the size of a large classroom or a small auditorium. There was a large map on one of the walls. It seemed appropriate because our prayer gathering consisted of two hundred people from various nations.

The map showed what Christian missions people call the 10/40 Window. The two numbers are latitude markings for the northern hemisphere. Between ten and forty-degree latitude lies a pathway of about seventy countries, ranging from northwest Africa to East Asia. Most of the world's Muslims, Hindus, and Buddhists live in this window. Christian missionaries have sought to share the gospel within this window, often resulting in their persecution and even death.

Our host, Operation Mobilization, was intent on attracting people to these mission endeavors. Operation Mobilization was cofounded by George Verwer, who became a Christian at a Billy Graham crusade in the 1950s. He passed away in 2023 after a lifetime of service on the mission field . The group's five thousand workers seek to build Christian communities worldwide and even use donated ships to do so.

Our prayer meeting was two hours long and "Korean style," meaning everyone prayed aloud and simultaneously. That was a new experience, so I watched with interest during the first few minutes. It was impressive and immersive. It wasn't chaotic; prayers were split among geographic areas where Operation Mobilization had a presence, often in hostile and dangerous parts of the world like the 10/40 Window.

Ushers passed through the audience handing out small white booklets, no more than eight or twelve pages in length. I quickly thumbed through and noted the different Operation Mobilization areas of emphasis. I paused at the section about the Dalits in India.

The Dalits, I learned, are known as "Untouchables"—a name they gave themselves out of shame. They sit at the bottom of the Indian caste system, invisible, despised, and regularly the victims of every human rights abuse. Even their shadows must be prevented from touching those of others. After drinking from a clay cup, a Dalit has to smash the cup to protect others from drinking from it. And because these people are so ignored, so devalued, they're prime targets for human trafficking.

I read these things, closed the booklet, and attempted to get my mind and heart back into the prayer meeting around me. But the Dalits continued to haunt me; I couldn't walk away and forget them—their shadows, broken cups, and broken people, predators coming to take them away and sell them, with no one caring.

I began to read more about them. I found that they often sold their children, but it was because they were told their children would be given better lives. "We'll educate them, feed them well," said the strangers. "They'll have the things you never could." But it was all a lie. They were selling their children into trafficking.

WIDE AWAKE

I was learning more about sex and labor trafficking in this world and how it was no small, isolated issue. It was a rampant contagion. I began to burn with rage. I watched documentaries, including short features by the Love146 group, a leader in fighting child trafficking.

Why the name Love146? These activists had seen victims reduced to numbers, as no one knows their names anymore: girls standing silently behind panes of glass, wearing identical red dresses, holding up ID numbers; buyers perusing restaurant-style menus listing various sex acts and prices. Something in the eyes of Girl 146 touched them deeply.

Human trafficking. Like most people, I'd heard the phrase but never given it deep thought; I was too busy with my life. Now I was awakening to what this thing meant.

A friend who had joined International Justice Mission helped bring me up to speed. I was overwhelmed—or perhaps a better phrase is *swept away* because suddenly death metal, electro-pop, and entrepreneurial strategies seemed insignificant in comparison to fighting trafficking.

I was recalling words Jesus had said about His fury toward those who *"despise...these little ones"* (Matthew 18:10). About how we are to treat *"the least of these"* (Matthew 25:40). And it was as if my own innocence abruptly ended.

I decided to find a way to help the Dalits of India by joining a nonprofit organization called Redeem the Shadows. Its name was inspired by the striking idea of the Dalits with their reviled shadows. While with the organization, our priorities quickly shifted. When we attended parties, we were the buzzkill because of our overzealous passion for fighting trafficking.

Around that time, Constella Chapters and Arms Embrace broke up, as bands do, but I wasn't entirely done with music. Performing onstage offered a platform for some of the anti-trafficking work I wanted to do. My sister Kristen and I began a new band called Anchor of Hope, an electronic rock group. Based on the European connections I'd gathered, we completed four European tours, during which we visited nineteen countries. We both wore anti-trafficking T-shirts on stage and discussed the issue for a minute or two during a break in each concert. We gave out flyers and sold shirts with our message as well.

Having this added purpose was meaningful to me. As for Kristen, she was more than ready to help fight trafficking—for reasons even more personal.

When Kristen was five and I was nine, our family went shopping at the town flea market. We walked together, my sister beside our parents, gazing at all the interesting objects for sale. Suddenly, a woman bumped into my dad. We all turned toward the woman instinctively, and the woman walked on. But my sister was gone.

It all happened quickly—a collision and a disappearance.

Dad's lightning response was astonishing. He told us to move quickly to a different exit, and we did. Dad chose the right one. He spotted a man hurrying toward the parking lot with my sister. He took off at a sprint toward them, shouting and pointing. This did the trick: the kidnapper abandoned Kristen and fled in panic.

That day is engraved in my mind—a man very nearly stealing my little sister forever. So when I first read about Dalit children at the prayer meeting, this event, with its raw emotions, came to the surface. It was my brush with trafficking, and I can only imagine Kristen's feelings about it. No one had to tell her how close she came to something unthinkable.

She and I spoke at our concerts, distributed our handouts, and sold a few T-shirts, but it wasn't enough to make me feel I was doing my part. The voice in my heart kept urging me to find some way to do more.

ON LOCATION

Stacey, a missionary from Operation Mobilization, helped us at our concerts in Europe by working the merchandise table or doing anything else we needed. She shared our passion for helping the Dalits. We'd talk about these things on tour, exchanging facts and updates.

One day, Stacey told me she had a friend named Priya in India whose parents ran a large ministry and orphanage. "Look, I say let's go there," Stacey said. "Priya is willing to host us. She could take us around, and we could finally see the Dalits in person."

I didn't need much convincing. As we talked and planned, we decided to make the most of the visit: we would film a documentary so others could see what we saw. I had learned so much from documentaries, and I was convinced that producing one was the best way to get the word out. We enlisted a German videographer/photographer named Reuben, and we flew to India in 2009, representing Redeem the Shadows. We spent three weeks filming and conducting interviews.

Priya made sure we got a complete picture of her home country, both its time-honored beauty and its unsightly scars. Her father pastored a large church that stayed busy meeting local needs, which were many. At first, I was surprised to find that a pastor could live in a five-story home, but soon, I understood why: the doors were open to the community. Anyone who showed up could be fed—hundreds of people, maybe even a thousand, during a day. This was much more than a house. It was a life raft in a sea of need.

We ventured away from the life raft, though. We visited crude mud huts, where we slept on the floor; once we even helped kill a chicken for a meal. We inspected trash heaps that served as homes and, of course, witnessed labor trafficking for ourselves. We saw people making shoes and other products for pennies in wages.

New Delhi, the capital, wasn't much better. We visited a brothel where kids were being trafficked. It was located just above a police station. There, on the second floor, girls stood pressing their faces against iron bars as people on the street studied them from below. Men inspected and selected them as they would meat at a butcher shop while a trafficker took their money. A police officer stood in the midst of them, keeping things calm as girls were being bought. It could get rowdy as people shouted each other down, trying to be the first to claim this girl or that one. As long as the traffickers kept their operation orderly and civil, the police did not interfere.

I looked to Priya, puzzled. "How can this happen?"

"There's a lot of corruption," she said. "The traffickers make it worth the police department's while to look the other way."

We got it all on film using a discreet camera in our vehicle. But Westerners tend to stick out, and our cover was soon blown. Perhaps a light glinted from our lens. A trafficker came charging toward our van, and we had to make a quick U-turn and leave. But much like the Love146 group, I'd focused on one face: a girl, perhaps fourteen years old, peering through the bars as men sized her up for purchase. She wore earrings and a dab of makeup. But I saw no fear; I saw no emotion of any kind. Her spirit had fled.

"One so young," I thought, "out of hope, out of caring." I wondered if there were any way our cameras could convey such a reality.

Priya introduced us to the mother of a thirteen-year-old boy who'd managed to escape his captors. He'd been promised gold and riches if he'd do as they told him. And for him, that meant helping his family. Of course, he agreed, not suspecting what his captors would demand of him. They took him away from his home city, and when he saw what he'd gotten into, he managed to make his getaway. But how could he get home without money for a train? Some kind man bought him a ticket, and when his mother met him at the station, she saw through her weeping that he'd been dressed like a girl.

That was an all-too-typical story, though it was one of few with a happy ending. There were just too many stories; the scale of this industry was staggering and soul-crushing. The three weeks we spent listening to these stories were some of my life's most draining and despairing. But I needed to hear every account. When I felt tempted to block out the gritty details, I forced myself to listen; I reminded myself that others had to *live* those experiences.

I could listen, let myself feel the outrage, and then use that outrage. I could use it as fuel for my talents, creativity, time, energy, social sphere, and every resource God gave me.

I was only one. But even one spark can ignite a flame.

4

OUR OWN BACKYARD

Travel changes people. And the greater the differential between home and destination, the greater the change.

India gave us plenty to ponder. We were emotionally exhausted from the shocking images and the tragic narratives of exploitation. Now, however, it was time to begin work on our documentary. The first step was a five-minute trailer. Our big idea then was to partner with Priya's family's ministry and orphanage. Together we would work to prevent young girls and boys from falling into the traps that lead to trafficking.

We got the short film put together, but that was as far as we advanced in our filmmaking plans. Changes within our nonprofit organization caused us to redirect our energy.

We decided to keep doing what we'd been doing: traveling. But now, we'd move through our home country and speak in churches, schools, and coffee shops. We'd get ourselves booked just as we did with our music, and we'd tell our stories and show our short film. Hopefully, we'd have plenty of opportunities to interact with individuals and enlist them in the fight against trafficking.

However, what began as a focus on India suddenly shifted to trafficking in the United States.

It happened in Houston, Texas. There, we met with an anti-trafficking group prepared to show us home-grown examples of what we'd seen on the other side of the world. There was a farm-to-market road with sites known for sexual solicitation. We decided to turn our trip from simple publicity to information-gathering for law enforcement.

For some reason, I thought I could walk around freely with a camera at such places, or at least take some snapshots. I thought I'd find a way to interview at least one girl on-site and learn what went on inside. I was much more naïve in those days.

We were driven to a brothel that was out in the open, looking like any other business. I walked up to the door. It seemed I needed to be buzzed in if I wanted to enter. I pushed the button, and once I was inside, I saw posted the same kind of "menu" as the ones in India—a full listing of sexual services with prices. I share more about the Houston trip in chapter five.

Though I'd seen these things before, I realized I had no idea what to do next. What was I going to say when approached? "Can I interview one of your victims?" wouldn't work. It occurred to me that I'd placed myself in a dangerous situation, so I turned and walked back to the vehicle.

"You're right," I told our hosts. "No attempt at hiding anything. But it doesn't seem smart to go any further."

We drove on, and our hosts pointed out various brothels. "This one traffics," said our host, coming to a specific location. "We're working with law enforcement on this next one," he said later. This group was heavily involved; they knew the territory and were pressuring officials to clean things up.

My trip to India had shown me what the problem looked like; this Houston trip showed me how near to home the problem was.

As disturbing as the situation was in India, where the police stood around and helped the traffickers maintain control, it still seemed like the far side of our planet. Houston, Texas, however, is a microcosm of America. It's filled with large churches. It's Southern. It's patriotic. Yet even there, you can order sexual exploitation from a menu.

DEFINING EVIL

Kristen and I still wanted to fight global trafficking. My journey had started with an international prayer meeting, the presence of maps, and a particular compassion for the Dalits of India. But Kristen's story began in America, in the very presence of her family. We began to theorize that most people we knew would be just as shocked as we'd been to learn the extent of human trafficking in the United States. Perhaps it made more sense for us to begin in our little corner of the globe instead of trying to take on the world.

This meant we'd need to continue public speaking and be very effective. Missionary-type slide shows and dull readings of statistics weren't going to accomplish much. We needed emotional impact, particularly for the church audiences we'd be addressing.

So, I began working to perfect our presentation. I was looking for the right words to express what evil was, and I came across the familiar quotation, "The only thing necessary for the triumph of evil is for good men to do nothing." It's often credited to Edmund Burke, though there's no evidence he ever actually said it; John Stuart Mill did say something similar. Wherever the saying originated, it's a good one, and I quote it regularly.

Every form of evil in our world occurs because people allow it to occur. We spend a great deal of time bemoaning the world's problems but very little time acting to solve them. I'm chasing after some of those "good men doing nothing." My goal is to get as many of them as possible to do *something*—even just a little bit. I believe every single one of us is capable of making a difference. After all, enough raindrops can wear down a mountain.

Of course, there's always been evil in the world. It's easy for each generation to believe it sees the worst, but perhaps it's mainly a case of more things being out in the light today. Nearly everyone carries a phone with a built-in camera that allows them to document all kinds of events. There are perhaps fewer dark alleys for evil to hide in today than there were in the past.

That's good. We know where the enemy is, and we just have to be willing to take up arms against him. This is true not only for my passion to disrupt trafficking, but also for injustice of various kinds.

Another belief of mine is that none of us are here simply to coast through life. Our time is but a shooting star. There's work to do, and while we have resources—time, strength, talents, or wealth—we should be putting them to work.

Initially, Kristen and I tried our best to do that, but we were still unfocused. Film or speaking tour? World or the United States? We finished our three-month awareness tour, and next on the docket was for Redeem the Shadows to open a safe house for trafficking victims here in this country. But we had no experience with red tape, which comes from every direction. It's a world of bureaucracy and endless forms, so those plans, too, fell by the wayside.

While we plotted our next moves, *Taken* became a big box-office hit. Liam Neeson was vastly outworking us in getting the message out, though his was a very Hollywood version of that message. Did people understand the problem was real and not some fictional story you see on a TV screen? I wasn't seeing nearly enough people coming forward to get involved. People were moving on to other subjects, as they do. Every issue has fifteen minutes of fame, it seems. I couldn't find any evidence of federal or state legislation, corporate involvement, or any other sign that our nation was ready to get serious about addressing trafficking—which meant it was going to keep growing as a "low risk" criminal industry.

I noticed this, however: technology was poised to explode. An information revolution was in progress. Where were these advances being put to work in the war against trafficking? Nowhere that I could see.

That was something for me to think about.

GETTING STARTED

I began to look for a place to effect change actively. I realized that the power to enact real change in communities is vested in our local governments. So, in 2013, I was appointed as Florida's anti-trafficking coordinator for the Department of Children and Families. I served in that role for a year, during which I continued to travel throughout my home state to visit secret safe houses. I also managed appropriations. Most importantly, I increased my understanding of trafficking, how law enforcement tends to fight it, and what problems arise.

I've already described my first raid and the unforgettable experience of moving through a hotel used for trafficking. That raid was a miniature education. It allowed me to see the preparation, planning, and intel gathering that goes on, as well as to witness how the victims are cared for. Seeing a successful rescue gave me a surge of hope.

I'll admit to experiencing a certain amount of youthful awe. I watched the team move around, all wearing ski masks, task force badges, and Kevlar vests, and I found myself wishing I could be clad in all that gear. It was one of the few times I wanted to be one of the "cool kids." Of course, I knew we weren't kids playing cops and robbers; it was just an amazing thing to observe, and I wanted to be a part of it.

The guy working at the hotel's front desk apparently tipped off the trafficker, which is common. When we entered the room, it was clear the perpetrator had taken off very quickly, leaving behind his clothes, jacket, shoes, and the girl alone in the corner, cowering in fright.

"I just want to go home to my family," she told us between tears.

She was over eighteen, and there was little we could do for her beyond arranging a bus ticket home, where her family awaited her. But it seemed clear she was safe, and I hoped and prayed that her parents and loved ones would give her the care and chance of recovery she needed.

One of the points that stood out for me was that the raid took place at a hotel. I was taken aback by the idea that such establishments would allow these crimes to take place on their premises and would protect the criminals instead of the victims. For that reason, Dark Watch works with litigators who target these hotels. It's another way of finding every possible angle to make the trafficker's job more difficult.

Another point of concern for me was the usual process non-government organizations must undertake. As someone who wanted to be part of the effort, I studied the mechanisms of their approach: raising awareness, raising money, helping victims through safe houses, and helping victims reintegrate into society. I get it. It's the Good Samaritan approach. You see someone wounded along the road, and you focus totally on helping them, paying their medical bills, and so on. That's an essential part of this war against trafficking, and I would never say a word against it. But the victim-centric approach doesn't necessarily engage the supply/demand reality of the crime. If an invasion force is attacking your village, you set up a medical unit, certainly—but you'd better do something about the barbarians at the gate, too.

I'm appreciative of everyone helping to fight trafficking, but sometimes we Samaritans need to go find the guy who beat up the victim by the side of the road. Otherwise, we're in the Band-Aid business.

GETTING TECHNICAL

I was interested in studying how our task force searched for traffickers. I was shocked to see them using Backpage.com, which was a website similar to Craigslist where people could post classified ads, but it was primarily known for soliciting prostitution. In 2018, the Justice Department shut down the site on one hundred counts of illegal sex solicitation.

Working from Backpage.com was an agonizingly slow and inefficient process. I figured there had to be a better way to use information technology to fight this crime. Anyone could simply work their way through these various hookup sites. This reaction was the genesis of Dark Watch.

I spoke with a computer programmer who had done computer coding for an intelligence agency. I asked him whether software could scan and automate the information on Backpage-type sites to speed up the process. He said, "Yes, of course." This is why we have computers—they can work through complex digital tasks faster than the human brain can.

"Can you help us?" I asked.

My new friend began bringing me up to speed on what was possible. He showed me the dark web, a corner of the World Wide Web located behind a series of hidden doors. It's on "overlay networks" and is accessible only through special software. The average user can't find these alleyways of cyberspace—but information specialists can. All kinds of illegal activities take place on the dark web. Drugs are bought and sold, fake passports are arranged, and murders are solicited. It's the ideal venue for exploitation and cybercrime.

My friend also acquainted me with something relatively new at the time: Bitcoin and cryptocurrency—financial transactions that supposedly left no tracks.

I was beginning to see just how complex and insidious this criminal world was, but at the same time, I knew that every strategy leaves some kind of vulnerability. He who lives by the Internet dies by it. So we worked nights and weekends to integrate some of the newest technology into our fight, beginning with algorithms and software processes that would rapidly analyze the information on pages like Backpage. For example, it wasn't difficult for a program to search out keywords that were associated with human trafficking. Phrases like "new in town foreign exchange student 200 roses" could mean that a child was being trafficked for $200 an hour.

The ways our field could use technology were limitless, yet few were tapping into it. So, after my state appointment ended, I turned to an old friend, a homeschooling debate partner from my teenage years. His name was Sam Curet, and he'd served as an intelligence officer in the Marines, including deployment in Afghanistan. He was pursuing a juris doctorate in law while working in corporate compliance and international real estate. Like me, he was passionate about stopping trafficking and had exceptional tech expertise. The Defense Intelligence Agency had recruited him to lead discussions on threat networks' activities in trafficking as an intelligence starting point.

I told Sam about traffickers advertising on Backpage, and he wasn't buying it. "No way," he said. "There's no way law enforcement wouldn't shut that down quickly. It's too easy a target."

"As you'll see, it is happening, and it's our starting point."

Sam pulled up the site, studied some of the ads, and was stunned that law enforcement made so few inroads when the criminal networks were hiding in plain sight. "There's all kinds of tech they could be using," he said, shaking his head. And I knew then he'd found the best place to use his skill set.

We cofounded Dark Watch in 2013, though under a different name. We developed analytical tools based on machine learning, providing high-quality intelligence to combat trafficking. We weren't out to make a name for ourselves—the whole point was to show the FBI and other organizations what could be done, share our tools, and then work closely with them. That didn't happen immediately. For the first two years we heard from groups that were curious about our techniques, but it never led to anything larger.

You might recall my college emphasis on entrepreneurship. While my heart was in this initiative to fight trafficking, my hands had to be busy elsewhere just to earn a living. I started a tiny-home business, tapping into the movement focused on downsizing living space. It was a hot trend at the time, and there were even two tiny-house television shows on the air. But my attempts in that direction didn't work out, any my business failed.

Next, I tried to transfer my interest in technology to the business sphere by accepting a position with a procurement tech company in Austin, Texas. After that, I went to work for a case management company in the same city, and then I was involved with a federal division of a high-resolution aerial imagery company. Add all these jobs to my musical career, and I was like the many-headed Hydra myself. But this is essential in entrepreneurship: you look for new markets with startup potential and hope to find one that takes off. So I was busy with my head(s) on a swivel.

Sam and I were beginning to feel that the Dark Watch idea was a case of failure to launch. Our approach made perfect sense to us, but what was it about this crime? Why was law enforcement so slow-moving and unambitious?

Just when we considering pulling the plug, our big break came at a Department of Defense showcase in 2017. There we made a presentation linking human trafficking and drug trafficking—a perfect example of the kind of analytics that needed to occur—and we made some inroads. Over the next couple of years, we saw a steady increase in Dark Watch. By 2019, we had received funding that allowed the two of us to leave our day jobs. By 2020, Dark Watch was going strong as a for-profit entity.

It was nice to focus on our venture, but I could also see how all those other jobs gave me valuable experience in preparation for what I was made to do. I recognized that it was a strange, curving road that brought me to that point. There was the early educational path that developed my curiosity and taught me to research everything for myself: The experience of watching my sister come within a few steps of being kidnapped. My rock group years that placed me in a prayer session where I learned about an abused caste in India, which planted seeds of compassion. My visit to India, which planted seeds of outrage and determination. Then, there was my cluster of work experiences, all of which helped me understand the business world and my strengths and weaknesses.

At just the right time, opportunities opened for Dark Watch—and we've since become a global leader in anti-trafficking intelligence. It's odd how, when we look back, twisted paths often seem like straight lines.

As I reviewed all these formative experiences, one other occasion came to mind, from when I was twelve years old. A friend and I were playing in the woods when some other kids began firing slingshots at people—with rocks. I knew nothing good could happen in that scenario, particularly since I had no slingshot to defend myself with. So I decided to leave the line of fire and go home. My friend saw things differently. Suddenly, he pulled out a knife and told me, "No, you're going to stay!"

He was my friend—at least up to that moment (though not afterward). It was an awful feeling to experience what it meant to be helpless under someone else's power.

We were just kids playing in the woods, and I doubt anyone would really have used a knife on me. But think about what trafficking victims feel. Trafficking isn't fun and games; the victims of trafficking are truly helpless. Someone is threatening them, saying, "You're going to stay," and forcing them to take part in terrible things. Yet all the victims want is to go home. Won't someone do something?

Now imagine living years of that life without rescue, and what it does to the human spirit: the utter loss of all hope and caring. The future tends to be drug addiction, severe mental and physical abuse, and an early death.

The existence of such abject darkness in my world bothers me too much to let me turn away. Whatever I can do, however little or much, I must do. I've found this cause to be worth giving my life to. I don't expect others to respond in the same way. But it would be nice to find a remnant of people who share my feelings that human trafficking is intolerable, that it can't be allowed, and who are willing to step forward and say, "I can help."

I hope this book finds its way to a few of those people.

5

A COMPLEX GLOBAL WEB

The subject matter in *Taken* was a shock to the public—as it was to me—to learn that slavery had reemerged from the shadows like a resilient cockroach and was evolving. This message needed to be spread far and wide. Once the public had taken in the terrible news, they began to learn about the depth and complexity of the problem. This problem is as deep and wide as the ocean.

The public was filled with new information, and that energized those of us working to fight trafficking. We were flooded with questions—mostly about what people could do to fight back. With this subject matter, it doesn't take much information to get people's full attention. Human trafficking is so revolting that nearly all of us want it stopped. But we must understand the problems first.

The early and loudest voices enlightening the public were organizations like International Justice Mission, Love146, and Not for Sale. November 11, 2011 (also known as 11.11.11, Redemption Day) was an effort to have artists and individuals all around the world hold up banners to raise awareness of this fight.

I began my work in the nonprofit sector as part of the growing effort to get the word out. But we needed to be at work at ground level, too. The team from Redeem the Shadows set up a three-month road trip with friends from churches and schools who felt drawn into the fight against human trafficking. It was a bit loose and spontaneous, but it was fueled by energy drinks, fast food, and our zeal to interact with people across America.

That van trip involved a lot of driving and being confined in an enclosed space with sweaty bodies. But it wasn't a joyride. We were dedicated to spreading the message far and wide. We moved from Florida to California by way of Texas, then back east through the Midwest, down through the Carolinas, and back to Florida, always open to any opportunity to talk with people about human trafficking. It was amazing and, of course, sad to see people's faces as, for the first time, they awakened to a new social tragedy.

It was exhausting, but we could point to places on the map where we'd initiated conversation, planted seeds, and engaged churches and communities. We could pray they'd grow into pockets of people determined not to look away from the problem. Just as I'd learned about the problem and started something new, maybe others would learn from our presentations and contribute their own creativity.

My niche in the fight was technology. I was becoming increasingly aware of the complexity of the criminal cobweb we were taking on. As a member of a younger generation that had grown up in a digital age, I could understand how we needed new tools to combat a new problem. After all, our opponents were savvy business entities. They knew the laws and regulations inside and out; they'd probed the weaknesses in our justice system, and they, too, were using technology to exploit those weaknesses. They even had a presence in the lobbying world, quietly campaigning to loosen laws that would impede their criminal interests.

In time, we met with the FBI and the Department of Homeland Security, which had all the political potential to adopt and use this data-driven approach on a much broader scale.

REVULSION, REACTION, RESPONSE

Sometimes, the popular response to problems is to look for a quick fix. People think that maybe they can solve this issue before their attention span runs out. (Probably not.) Perhaps they can just make a small financial contribution somewhere. (At least it's a start.)

Of course, much more is needed for large problems—vastly more. Human trafficking is a large problem, a global problem, and a criminally protected problem. As we mentioned earlier, the typical response is victim-centric; we focus on healing the one we've rescued. This is necessary, but it's like putting out a fire without going after the arsonist—which is the hard part.

We need a tough mindset, a multidirectional attack, and a focus on the criminals themselves. That means updated technology and a legal tool set. In some cases, we need to work for new laws and amend existing laws on the local and federal levels to eliminate the loopholes and weak spots that traffickers exploit. We must be well-informed at the ground level, city to city and issue to issue.

Of course, this doesn't mean paying less attention to the victims. We know now that victims' lives tend to be cut short due to physical stress, addiction, and abuse that occurs within the trafficking experience. According to the nonprofit Phoenix Rising, from the moment someone enters the captivity of trafficking, they have on average seven more years to live.[4] And we're talking, largely, about young people.

---

4. "What is Human Trafficking," About Trafficking, Phoenix Rising KY, https://phoenixrisingky.org/about-trafficking, accessed April 22, 2024.

The film *Taken* inspired me. Liam Neeson's character heroically saved the day in just over ninety minutes using a "unique set of skills." I fantasized about developing those skills myself, going out into the field, and dealing out justice to these predators.

But then I saw a few situations in real life. In Houston, Texas, in a sex-trafficking brothel, I realized that no Hollywood movie can capture the dimensions of this issue. How many houses like this are there in Texas? In the United States? In the world? How many new ones will open while we're dealing with this one? It's dizzying; it feels like stopping a waterfall with a spoon. In Texas, it's a felony to solicit sex, and we have gigantic, glaring signs that advertise the fact. Yet, as you drive along, you'll see people engaging in the sex trade right beneath those very signs.

Discouragement is one of our most dangerous opponents, but facts come to the rescue: I don't have to carry on this fight alone. I don't have to visit every site. I don't have to go into battle without weapons. My weapons are technological and judicial.

THE FACES OF TRAGEDY

FM 1960 in Houston sounds like a radio station, but it actually refers to Farm to Market Road 1960, which skirts the north end of the city, moving through places like Humble, Texas, and serves as the superhighway of human trafficking in the area. Most urban areas have such a road or sector. One late night, I was sitting in a van with a local nonprofit representative who helped me access the target. It was a fact-finding mission for me: get in, find out pricing, identify victims, and get out again with helpful intelligence. We'd then take that information to local law enforcement.

I walked into the building and faced a plate glass window. The victims stood on the opposite side of the window, mere inventory. Prices were posted as they might be in the meat section at a grocery store. I was supposed to select a victim and begin a conversation, but I froze despite my need to blend in and gather intel. The words just stuck in my throat.

All my training and preparation, and I had no clue what to say. The empty gazes facing me undercut my ability to follow a script.

I tried memorizing some of the prices—and, painfully, the faces—and left. For the moment, I felt helpless. But the deep-seated fury took hold and became the seed for what I *could* do: begin work on technology that would eventually track thirty-thousand illicit and illegal crime establishments like the one I saw in Texas.

These places are easy to find in our cities. They're located along neglected thoroughfares, in faded strip malls, or perhaps even in suburbia. But they successfully defy opposition because of the "shell game" their sponsoring corporations play. In organized crime, shell corporations are the best cover imaginable. These are businesses created simply to direct financing while hiding the source. They're not generally illegal in concept, but they're easy to abuse.

At the same time, criminal elements move traffic rapidly through these venues, in such numbers and so quietly that law enforcement simply can't keep up. We tend to underfund our police—particularly on the sides of town where these sex shops pop up. In Houston, I didn't do anything the police couldn't have done, but the police had too many pressing needs elsewhere.

But what if we could cut out some of the time traditionally required to track down the offenders? Technology offers speed and efficiency. What if our Dark Watch maps could gather valuable information quickly, at low cost, and without law enforcement having to assign a task force? What if our web tracing tools could reveal the hidden identities of human traffickers by using databases and identifiers to suggest the most likely suspects?

We've built our programs and processes to find and gather evidence on the criminals who have defied intervention in the past.

This doesn't solve every problem—organized crime has access to computers, too—but it evens the playing field and tips the scales of justice in our favor.

THE FENTANYL FACTOR

My continued involvement in this fight provided opportunities to listen to the stories of survivors of sex trafficking. These stories were always sad and infuriating at the same time, and each one is utterly heartbreaking in its own way. I continue to be surprised by victims' entanglements with other problems—particularly narcotics.

Some of the survivors are victims of organized crime; others have been trafficked by their family members, generally to support a drug habit, such as an opioid addiction. The role of addiction in all this is a complicating factor.

Earlier in the book, I told the story of the young lady we helped free, who leaped from a van to run into her father's arms—a prodigal daughter came home. Yet within two hours, her system began to cry out for fentanyl. That's the narcotic of choice for ensnaring victims in this trade.

Fentanyl is a national crisis all in its own, but when it crosses over into trafficking, our work of liberation becomes exponentially more difficult. We had this young lady in safe arms, free from her captors—right where she wanted to be. But the desire to feed her addiction overwhelmed every other drive within her. She would have done nearly anything to get that fix, including running back into danger. And what about the next victim? What about those who might never try to run, so furious is their need for the next dose?

Fentanyl is a synthetic opioid that was originally used as a pain medication reserved for extreme situations, such as patients suffering from various cancers. But it escaped the loose confines of the pharmaceutical world and has now become a worldwide killer. Typically flowing into the United States via the southern US border, it was responsible for 70,000 of the 106,000 drug-related deaths in 2021.[5]

A lethal dose of fentanyl is so small you might not even see, taste, or smell it. Celebrities like Lil Peep, Mac Miller, Coolio, Tyler Skaggs, Michael K. Williams, Prince, and Tom Petty all died of overdoses and complications that involved fentanyl. A powerful drug called Narcan is often the only thing that can save an individual exposed to too much of the killer drug.

So we need to understand that in our time, we've seen the explosion of both sex trafficking and drug trafficking, and it's inevitable that the two form a dark entanglement. Both have the same result: a blow to the victim that is very difficult to survive—physically, mentally, emotionally, and spiritually.

On the occasions that we do manage to rescue someone from this depth of bondage, the real work is still ahead. People are devastated. It's just possible that, like the young lady in our story, they feel overwhelmed, hopeless, and ready to return to the trafficker at any moment. Our determination to restore and redeem must be greater than the power of drugs, shame, despair, and every other dark power. We need the grace and power of God.

OTHER CHALLENGES

One of the issues we face is characterized by bitter irony: We rescue people who have become accustomed to roaming the streets in the early hours of the morning, smoking and drinking. It feels like some kind of freedom, though it's quite the opposite. Now, pulled out of that nightmare world and relocated to a safehouse,

---

5. National Institute on Drug Abuse, "Drug Overdose Death Rates," National Institutes of Health, June 30, 2023, https://nida.nih.gov/research-topics/trends-statistics/overdose-death-rates#:~:text=.

they feel trapped, confined, and denied the substances that rule their nervous systems.

Some safehouses lock up survivors with a television and a Netflix account, counting on time alone to perform some miracle. This method feels like imprisonment, and it's not enough. The best rehabilitation programs I've seen are family-based—survivors are placed with families that are willing and patient enough to foster trafficked victims. We call these often faith-based programs *micro-rehabilitation*. The human element of caring is a powerful curing agent. But as you can imagine, there are only so many homes willing to take in someone damaged by this process, and even then, there's still a high risk of the victim taking flight and returning to the abuse, even knowing they will face a violent reception for having run away.

Now, imagine this twist: victims showing up at a safehouse as a way to recruit others for the trade. It happens. Some people, perhaps with Stockholm syndrome, fully accept what has become their daily life. They're recruited by traffickers to join in the operations and to recruit others out in the street. Sometimes this involves going into recovery programs under false pretenses so that they can find the weakest and most vulnerable and bring them into the trafficker's network.

Despite the layers of complexity to this issue, there are individuals and nonprofit organizations that redouble their efforts to fight the trafficking industry, and they have my utter respect. The International Justice Mission is one example; this organization brings a global attack to a neighborhood-to-neighborhood fight.

International efforts are sometimes easier than those in the United States. That's because of the approach used to prosecuting these cases in the United States. Prosecutors have the difficult task of building cases against traffickers. They rely on a survivor's testimony. But under the pressure of cross-examination, a traumatized victim is likely to make mistakes, misremember details, and not appear credible to a jury. All of this leads to cases being thrown out and traffickers going back to work with greater impunity. They scoff at the inability of the US justice system to stop what they're doing.

That's frustrating to me. Hearing the victim's story is essential, and I'm sure prosecutors think they're doing a good thing by giving them a voice. However, victims struggle with shame, and placing them in the witness box and submitting them to interrogation adds insult to injury.

Cases in Florida have been thrown out because of violation of search and seizure laws, improperly cleared surveillance, or some other procedural misstep by agents of justice. District attorneys are aware of all these problems as well as the lack of credible witnesses and evidence in sex trafficking testimony. Since prosecutors focus on the most winnable cases, sex trafficking charges are often thrown out, dismissed, or pushed away.

The sex trafficking industry has taken the shape of our prosecution issues in some ways. The offenders understand where the problems are, and they've built their empire within the limitations of the laws of the justice system. As I began to understand this, I realized the only way to fight back was to attack from new directions and with better weapons. If the law had loopholes, surely the criminals did, too.

Specialized technology wouldn't fill every gap, but I knew it could fill some. But even more than that, the approach needed to change. The key goals had to focus on the criminals rather than their victims, the data about them rather than what a witness might or might not remember, and an effort to provide these tools to law enforcement officers who could use them with much better efficiency.

EXPLOITING VULNERABILITIES

The US War on Drugs began, formally speaking, in 1971 during a press conference by President Richard Nixon. More than half a century later, there were few significant victories. But that war created a framework for using RICO and racketeering laws to prosecute drug traffickers. It's a way of attacking the most vulnerable part of the criminal enterprise, if not the most obvious.

Most people know that the gangster Al Capone was caught through tax evasion charges. His crimes were far more significant on other fronts, but he was well-insulated from accountability in those directions, so his tax record became his downfall. In the 1990s, crime syndicates were driven from New York City through racketeering statutes. In the cases of Capone, organized crime, or traffickers of various kinds, it's possible to show financial gain without tax payment.

In human trafficking, a dual-track prosecution uses victim testimony (the traditional approach) but also evidence of money laundering, racketeering, and conspiracy to commit fraud. These tracks leave paper trails that witnesses aren't able to offer. So, the human, emotional story is told through the victims, while the more effective prosecution comes through the exposure of financial crime.

Here's where the Dark Watch approach enters the equation. We know that the use of the Internet creates a digital footprint. It may seem intangible compared to a contract on paper, but paper can easily be hidden, locked away, or destroyed. Practical digital forensic work will find and preserve the goings-on in cyberspace. If you visit a website of any kind, use a GPS app on your phone, or make a cash transaction, that data is captured. Each of us has a unique digital footprint online.

Sex traffickers are no exception. They may rely on online marketplaces to promote their services. I've already referred to our experiences with Backpage, where we found that people were for sale among the tables and chairs, cars, and valuable baseball cards. (Craigslist removed its "adult services" section in 2010, at which time many of the traffickers moved over to Backpage.)

I discussed the problem with agents at the FBI and other law enforcement agencies. Some felt the clear response was to take down Backpage, using federal power, and seize the assets. But there was another view, and it went like this: Why not leave it in place, sit back, and allow the criminals to give us information about themselves we might not get otherwise? This is the equivalent of having their business report delivered to our front door. Let's use it to garner intelligence rather than kill it.

And for a time, that's what we did. But in 2018, the US government decided this was also the criminals delivering their enticements to the victims' door; the site had to be taken down. A ninety-three count indictment was brought against the site owners, arguing that modern-day slavery was facilitated by this website. Victims testified in support; one of them was a fifteen-year-old who had been trafficked.

This case paved the way for the congressional bills known together as FOSTA-SESTA. FOSTA is the somewhat confusing short name for the Allow States and Victims to Fight Online Sex Trafficking Act; SESTA is the Stop Enabling Sex Traffickers Act. The breakthrough was on how Internet publication could be handled legally, and obviously, the repercussions echoed across the online world. FOSTA-SESTA clarified that we could sue online platforms that facilitate human trafficking.

This did not mean that the war was won. In the absence of Backpage, the Hydra again spawned many heads to replace the one cut off. More websites began to carry the bait put out by criminal networks. This shows how lucrative human trafficking is—it's worth the risk of being brought to justice, of suffering the fate of Backpage. Indeed, those who run the networks may have learned from that case. They may be more clever in their pitches, but there are hundreds of escort services concealing offers of illegal sex. Use of the dark web isn't even necessary; the "surface web" (aka clear web), which most of us use every day, can host these listings.

But Dark Watch has grown more clever as well. Working with former intelligence agents and current technologists, we built tools to scour the Internet for keywords, images, and phrases that usually constitute the footprints of the traffickers. From there, our analysts can track the locations and operations of these traffickers, allowing us to begin to accumulate evidence that can be used in human trafficking cases. I've been pleased to see our technology result in arrests and indictments.

TARGETING SPONSORS

If we've used the law books to exploit the vulnerabilities of the traffickers, we've also gotten better at going after the more prominent industries that facilitate their work—what we could call "sex traffic-adjacent" businesses.

For example, it may not be surprising that the massive pornography industry is tied in with trafficking. It's possibly more eye-opening to consider that major sporting events also have connections to it. In both cases, expensive and powerful lobbyists work hard to deny these facts. Any exposed sex trafficking is just coincidence, they say; it's not an actual problem but "consensual sex work."

We follow where the facts lead, however, and we're becoming more successful at demonstrating the depth of the ties between these industries and trafficking. As of the writing of this book, Pornhub was the fifteenth most viewed website in the world. It's part of a whole network of online pornography. In 2022, a group of sex trafficking victims sued Pornhub under the FOSTA-SESTA acts that were established in 2018, when Backpage was taken down. Those congressional bills are offering tools so that mass tort litigators, skilled lawyers, and personal injury firms can go after sponsors that have in the past been immune: hotel chains, social media sites, gaming sites, and other industries that have a lot of public goodwill at stake.

Our hope is that they will no longer be able to look the other way and rely on deceptive lobbyists. The idea of "constructive knowledge" is becoming an effective weapon. In other words, we're not just responsible for what we know; we're responsible for what we *should have* known. Business leaders are responsible for what goes on during their watch if it can reasonably be shown that the actions were prominent or repetitive. They are accountable. This opens up possibilities for civil suits and criminal charges that become expensive for the accused.

Activist groups object. They claim "legitimate sex work" is unfairly impacted by FOSTA-SESTA enforcement. But we're beginning to see larger victories over sex trafficking. In the Deutsche Bank case we mentioned earlier, victims were awarded $75 million. In 2023, at least forty lawsuits were carried forward against large hotel chains that "should have known" how their facilities were being used.

Will any of this serve as deterrence for sex trafficking, or will perpetrators simply regroup and find new strategies? Undoubtedly, holding industries accountable—travel, hospitality, social media, banking, food and beverage, and others—will, at the very least, create obstacles for the criminals responsible. We encounter the complexity of the industry we're fighting, which is entangled with many other industries. We must follow every trail, stay current, and come up with holistic solutions.

Even as you read this chapter, the masterminds of trafficking are devising new plans. But you can be sure we're mobilizing more ways to fight back.

6

ACROSS CULTS AND CULTURES

Specific images come to mind when we hear the term *human trafficking*—very disturbing images. But it refers to a broad category that encompasses at least three areas: sex, labor, and human organs. All these involve force, fraud, and coercion, the basic elements we must demonstrate to establish this category. And in the end, it's all about buying and selling. If drugs and weapons can be trafficked, so can people.

About 15 percent of trafficking cases in the United States involve labor trafficking. Unfortunately, these cases are difficult to identify. For example, about a third of the estimated ten thousand labor trafficking cases in the United States involve domestic servants, and those cases are often ignored.[6] In any case, most of the emphasis is placed on sex trafficking. But forced labor is found in a significant number of occupations, sometimes involving children. In other cases, it's tightly tied to sex trafficking.

Organ trafficking may be even less familiar to us than labor trafficking. Across the world, there's great demand for healthy

---

6. National Institute of Justice, "The Prevalence of Labor Trafficking in the United States," February 26, 2013, nij.ojp.gov: https://nij.ojp.gov/topics/articles/prevalence-labor-trafficking-united-states.

human internal organs, usually for transplant surgery, and there are never enough suitable hearts, livers, kidneys, or other organs available. When parts are sold for a profit or transacted out of the mainstream medical system, this is classified as organ trade or trafficking. A donor might be paid as little as $1,000 for a kidney, but it will be sold for five times that.[7]

Sex trafficking is the most common of the three forms of trafficking, and it is the form most tied in with organized crime. More often than the other forms, sex trafficking hides in plain sight in typical American communities through livestream commercial sex videos, pornography, commercial sex, illicit massage brothels, and forced marriage scenarios. Most of this is categorized under what lobbyists have assigned the morally dubious label "legitimate sex trade" (for example, voluntary participation in those videos or massage brothels).

In many cases, however, the participants in these trades are under the control of others who farm them out for profit.

In this chapter, we examine how raids, social media, cults, and the power of coercion are involved with trafficking.

RAIDS

A raid is enacted when there's an opportunity to uncover an operation amid action, thus providing smoking-gun evidence. These large-scale operations can be risky and must be performed with strict adherence to search and seizure and other laws, but sometimes the result is the rescue of large numbers of children and adult victims, and the arrest of their captors.

One of the most extensive raids on record is one coordinated by Interpol, the International Criminal Police Organization, in 2016. It is known as Operation Intercops, and its targets were in

7. Clare Nullis-Kapp, "Organ trafficking and transplantation pose new challenges," *Bulletin of the World Health Organization*, 82 (9), 715, https://iris.who.int/handle/10665/269242.

South and Central America. In the end, authorities rescued more than 2,700 victims. Just as significantly, there were 134 arrests, and at least seven organized crime networks were dismantled. This is comparable to arresting major drug traffickers rather than just users. The destruction of the criminal networks exponentially redeemed more than 2,700 lives in one raid. The future of this cartel was cut off.

These raids, while impressive, are the tip of the iceberg; the world is facing a massive problem, the stakes are high, and many thousands of lives are in danger. If the crime is cut out at the roots, then many victims can be saved, and criminals can be brought to justice.

But what preparations must precede such a raid? First, there must be international cooperation between countries to conduct it. Interpol has 196 partner countries and does a good job navigating the different legal and enforcement standards among them. Operation Intercops involved twenty-five partnering countries gathering and sharing information on organized crime syndicates, traffickers, and gangs. It helped that all the nations involved were eager to eliminate the scourge of trafficking from their home countries.

Once the countries have agreed, Interpol must determine the primary language to use in communications, arrange translators, and select standard technology; this is often no small challenge. Some countries have progressed far more than others in basic computer systems. For example, imagine the latest Windows computer coordinating with one of the earliest Windows systems.

Actionable intelligence is the holy grail of information. This is the information that will stand up to any challenge in the methods of surveillance, arrest, or prosecution. It has to be gathered correctly. It must be solid and indisputable. This necessary precision means that an Interpol raid can take years in the planning and operation, but it's worthwhile. Of the 2,700 lives saved in the

Intercops raid, twenty-seven were teenage girls subjected to sex and labor trafficking.

It began with the knowledge that gold mining in certain areas tends to rely on slave labor taken from poverty-stricken populations. In Peru, nine hundred officers operated in the gold mining town of La Rinconada.

Interpol dismantled the notorious Paniagua network, which supported a global slavery chain that moved women between Colombia and China. A Colombian villager, not even comprehending what was ensuing, could find themselves enslaved thousands of miles from home in China for a life of sexual abuse and imprisonment. Breaking up such an ongoing arrangement is a goal that motivates all of us.

Other discoveries are equally appalling. In Honduras, Interpol partners came across a two-year-old orphan being trafficked. In that country, children are literally robbed from the cradle and sold for illegal adoption. Several agencies around the world are willing to exploit the desire and impatience of parents who want to adopt, and the procurement of infants becomes lucrative and, in some places, not too difficult.

Labor trafficking is exposed as well. In Bolivia, a company was shut down for promising high-paying jobs that led only to enslavement with no pay at all. One of the most hopeful features of the bust was that Bolivian authorities were able to conduct an awareness campaign, telling citizens how to protect themselves from trafficking in the future. Education is one of our best weapons for curbing these crimes in the future.

Interpol's Operation Intercops was a particularly fruitful enterprise, and fortunately it was not a one-time effort. Each year, the agency continues to conduct raids and bring traffickers to justice.

SOCIAL MEDIA

Social media has become a central element, even a driving element, of modern culture. We think of Facebook, Instagram, X (formerly Twitter), TikTok, and other social media outlets as casual hang-outs: places to carry on conversations, share vacation pictures, or see what's happening. But these are also predatory environments for traffickers who go wherever the people are—particularly the young people.

BBC News Arabic recently found a case of domestic workers being bought and sold on Instagram. Women were marketed online, and their pictures were displayed on the app to help customers make buying decisions on their phones. The pictures were sorted by race and other distinctions, and a typical purchase might cost a few thousand dollars.[8]

As with hotel chains and other businesses linked to trafficking, social media companies, worth billions of dollars, can be called out and held accountable for how their sites are used. Facebook, Google, and Apple immediately set in motion policies and practices to eliminate black market activities on their sites. But even with all their top-level tools, they've found it difficult to keep the traffickers out.

Social media programs rely on complex algorithms that employ user data to determine what users see in their feeds. Traffickers use the algorithms to promote their content higher and higher so it may be seen even when someone is looking for something else.

Consider that 5.7 million children use social media.[9] Children, of course, are naïve and often trusting of strangers, and traffickers on sites such as Snapchat know how to target them. The criminals

---

8. Owen Pinnell and Jess Kelly, "Slave markets found on Instagram and other apps," *BBC*, October 31, 2019, https://www.bbc.com/news/technology-50228549.

9. Sagul Ali, "Human Traffickers Use Social Media to Target Children," *Hayes Hall Gazette*, January 24, 2021, https://desis.osu.edu/seniorthesis/index.php/2021/01/24/human-traffickers-use-social-media-to-target-children.

might impersonate a friend, a loved one, or another child. These sites are being used to groom future victims. These vulnerabilities are currently being studied carefully, but the best safeguard is for parents to monitor and restrict their children's online activities.

CULTS ENTER THE PICTURE

As we review stories of trafficking, we see the faces of the victims, if only in our mind's eye. We can imagine hurting, exploited children, young girls, or Colombian peasants who don't quite understand how they got where they are. I think of that first raid in which I participated, and the face of the girl cowering in the corner of a hotel room. So much life and spirit had drained from her eyes.

But what about the faces of the traffickers? Who are they? How would we recognize one if we met them face to face? We wouldn't, of course. They seem to remain in the shadows, ill-defined, particularly as we find ourselves focused on and compassionate toward the victims. What drives these criminals to the unthinkable depravity of destroying human lives for profit?

It's not difficult to look up one or two of them; perhaps there's one located a few blocks from your home. I live in a pleasant neighborhood consisting primarily of retirees and families. Yet I know where the illicit massage brothels are—several of them. These are moving across America more rapidly than Starbucks stores. We recognize them by the blacked-out windows, the "open till midnight" posted hours, and the evidence that people live on the premises. We can walk into these parlors, ask to see the manager, and look into the eyes of a trafficker who may seem like any other hardworking businessperson.

Or we can look toward the red carpet, glossy world of celebrity culture. Take Andrew Tate, for example. He came to fame as a kickboxer and then as an attention-grabbing cast member of the UK's version of the *Big Brother* reality show. By appealing to those interested in hypermasculinity and machismo, he became an icon for those weary of feminism and any moral restraint around women.

Tate created "Hustler University" to promote modern wealth through online businesses. His TikTok videos were viewed over 11.6 billion times, and he had 4.6 million followers on Instagram. Unfortunately, he also employed his charisma and market savvy nature in his work as an alleged human trafficker.

The vast majority of his following, quite predictably, comprised younger males. Parents began noticing disturbingly aggressive and abusive behavior among their sons, who were devoted to Tate. In December of 2022, Tate was arrested in Romania for rape, trafficking, and forming an organized crime group, along with three other individuals. His main "hustle," allegedly, was pornography using coerced victims; the investigation and arrest came after a Romanian man called the authorities and said his ex-girlfriend was being held captive in the home Tate and his brother shared. Other women then came forward to accuse him of a standard technique used by pimps: seducing women for what seems like a romantic relationship but becomes forced sex work. RICO/racketeering laws were being added to sex trafficking charges. Andrew Tate has pleaded innocent to these charges, and as of 2023, investigations for money laundering and trafficking of minors were in progress.

Andrew Tate makes one wonder if the celebrities we see pushing a selfish and hedonistic view of sexuality are one more face of trafficking.

The word *culture* comes from the same root as *cult*, which in Latin means "worship." Culture takes in who we are as a society, what we care about, our art, our customs. In other words, what we worship, whether we think of it in those terms or not. Celebrity culture indeed approaches some modern form of elevated devotion, and cults form around figures such as Tate, as they do with rap singers or movie stars.

Another sex trafficking cult formed around Keith Raniere, who led the NXIVM cult (pronounced *NEX*-ee-um). He had spent the 1980s building wealth through the Amway multilevel marketing system and decided to build his business empire. Raniere, along with his associate Nancy Salzman, a former psychiatric nurse, used network marketing techniques to find victims. The group presented itself as a self-help organization based near Albany, New York. Its Executive Success Program and other workshops attracted an estimated eighteen thousand enrollees who were starved for wealth and prominence. Raniere was personally idolized in the same manner as Andrew Tate. He was known to his followers as "Vanguard" and particularly noted for his strong integrity and sense of ethics.[10]

Yet within the cult was a secret society, which lured seven hundred victims, including several people who were celebrities themselves. Members were told to provide nude photographs, and these provided blackmail ammunition (sextortion) in the event of someone backing out. Allison Mack was the head recruiter. She was an actress from the hit TV show *Smallville* and another show called *The Following*, about a super-criminal who led a cult of believers who served him slavishly. The well-known heirs to a liquor company fortune bankrolled much of these activities.

Victims were branded with Raniere's initials and commanded to have sex with him. Inevitably, a few came forward (one being fifteen years old) to report the branding and the forced sex. On October 27, 2020, Raniere was found guilty and sentenced to 120 years of prison and fined $1.75 million.

In the aftermath, people pointed to the role of social media in facilitating the exploitation of massive numbers of people. Currently the United States is torn between First Amendment freedom of speech and the abuses of it that lead to so many social

---

10. Will Yakowicz, "When We Exposed Keith Raniere, The Leader of the Nxivm 'Sex Cult,'" *Forbes*, May 15, 2019, https://www.forbes.com/sites/willyakowicz/2019/05/15/keith-raniere-the-leader-of-the-nxivm-sex-cult/?sh=79d3084635a9.

problems. As lawsuits target the websites and the massive companies that run them, we can only expect them to take more responsibility over what goes on in their sections of cyberspace. As always, ethics causes discussion, finance and market share cause action.

POWER, FORCE, AND COERCION

What can we learn from these scandals, which, if they hadn't happened, wouldn't have been considered believable enough for a movie script?

Both of Raniere's cults used social media. Digging deeper, we see an appeal to power and wealth that plays on people's dreams and their darker impulses. "You can have everything you want" is the message; X (formerly Twitter) and Instagram are the messengers. Millions of people are seduced by the artificial images larger-than-life celebrities have created of themselves. Who wants to be a millionaire? Nearly everyone. There is no law against that.

But from these pools of hopeful people are drawn victims for exploitation and abuse. People are attracted by the idea of more power, only to be stripped of their power. They're promised financial freedom, only to have their freedom stolen from them.

The two cult scenarios are extreme examples. There are other, less extreme occasions when traffickers use kidnapping, brute force, or other cruder means to build their inventory of victims. For instance, there's the "Romeo" scam, in which someone feigns personal romantic interest in a target and ultimately ensnares them like cattle. Other times, fentanyl is used to dope victims and keep them addicted. And, of course, there's the sextortion strategy, which exploits the trend of people sending nude pictures of themselves through texting. Those pictures are then used for blackmail purposes. "Come in, take a few pictures for us, and we'll destroy those originals." More compromising blackmail material is then produced, and the victim may be caught up in sex trafficking.

Social media only makes the process a little easier. It draws in certain types of people—people with vulnerabilities—creating a database of likely victims.

Whatever the strategy, Christian groups are drawn to fighting trafficking because they believe all people are God's creation and have eternal value. Believers in Jesus Christ are God's beloved children, part of His flock. Jesus said, *"I am the good shepherd; I know my sheep and my sheep know me…I lay down my life for the sheep"* (John 10:14–15). They believe Jesus's claim that He came *"to set the oppressed free"* (Luke 4:18) and respect His warning that *"If anyone causes one of these little ones…to stumble, it would be better for them to have a large millstone hung around their neck and to be drowned in the depths of the sea"* (Matthew 18:6). Human trafficking is an intolerable violation of everything the Christian faith stands for, and we have no choice but to wipe it out.

Trafficking, then, has three main types but infinite variations and combinations. It can be tied in with all kinds of industries, it can happen anywhere, and it will use whatever means are available, from brand new technology to age-old human desires. But we find it by "following the money," as Bernstein and Woodward advised in *All the President's Men*. Finance is the controlling factor because money is the reason for it. People will do anything as long as it makes them money and the price is paid by someone other than themselves. And profit margin is also the path toward getting corporations to eliminate it when it encroaches on their territory.

This is what we do in our fight. We follow the money, which often leads us overseas to countries we've never visited or thought much about. It places us in the path of criminal syndicates we thought were confined to Hollywood gangster movies. It leads us deep into the dark web and out again into the clear web, and it carries us into the realms of weapons, drugs, terrorism, political corruption, and any other place where money can be made.

The sum of $150 billion annually makes for quite an industry, and its size and lucrative nature does nothing to expose it in public. Instead, it buys a lot of invisibility. If organized crime's big move at the end of the last century was toward narcotics, it's toward human trafficking in this one. Federal and local laws are trying to catch up and adjust to the need for anti-trafficking legislation. Detection and prevention techniques are still being created and polished. Encryption, cryptocurrency, and artificial intelligence are examples of newer technology that will offer new opportunities for traffickers—but hopefully for their opponents as well.

Here's one example of a problem we wouldn't have even imagined a few years ago: What if artificial intelligence fabricated a sex video of an individual engaged in nonconsensual sex? The artist is a computer. Who is responsible for the crime, and how is the crime classified for prosecution? Can artificial intelligence be used to throw off the pursuit of criminals?

We won't have all the answers anytime soon. What we can do, however, is stay abreast of the latest technology, keep informed of the newest trends in trafficking, attract as many people as possible to help us in the fight—and then pray that the goodness and mercy of God is the deciding factor. *"The light shines in the darkness, and the darkness has not overcome it"* (John 1:5).

7

ORGAN TRAFFICKING

Daniel came to London in May of 2022. BBC News called him Daniel; his real name was withheld because he still lived in fear, even though the immediate danger was behind him.

Daniel was a street trader in Lagos, Nigeria. From his cart he sold accessories for cell phones—cases, mostly. One day he was approached by a stranger and asked how he would like the opportunity of a lifetime: to travel to the United Kingdom to work.

It seemed clear to Daniel that this was a job offer. From his vantage point, a British job of almost any kind would be superior to his daily struggles in impoverished Nigeria. He didn't find it odd when he was told that taking a blood test was the only prerequisite for the passport that would make his travel possible.

In reality, the stranger was checking Daniel's health to ascertain whether his kidney could be removed.

Daniel enjoyed his flight to London, though he found it odd that he was given no access to his passport or any extra spending money to tide him over. His sponsors watched him and gave him strict orders about what to do and where to stay. They were extremely concerned with getting Daniel into the country physically and keeping him from wandering away.

Daniel, who could speak only a little English, was anxious to learn about his new job. He received no answers to his questions, but he was introduced to a young Nigerian woman named Sonia Ekweremadu, who was in her mid-twenties, just like him. The daughter of a powerful Nigerian politician, she told him she had a severe kidney disease, had to undergo five-hour dialysis sessions three to four times per week, and was desperate for Daniel to donate his kidney to her.

Daniel was to be presented as her cousin, a willing organ donor. Otherwise he was to answer "no" to each of a series of questions he would be asked. (Later, Sonia's father explained that he had been deceived and had no idea how the kidney would be procured. At trial, Sonia was found innocent of wrongdoing.)

Things became even more confusing. Daniel found himself in a small room at the Royal Free Hospital in London, frantically using the few English words in his vocabulary to find out what would be done to him. The doctors were talking about the risks of a kidney removal operation. They gave him a little talk about the lifelong medical care that he would need. Before that day, there had been no suggestion that he be a donor.

As they spoke, it all became clear to Daniel. The rosy hopes he had been cherishing vanished into the antiseptic air of the hospital room. There was no job; it was indeed a "life-changing adventure," if not the type he imagined. This was all about extracting his kidney and giving it to a stranger. His hosts didn't seem to care what happened to him after he'd been operated on and sewn up.

The doctors, who were not part of the arrangement, recognized Daniel as a confused young man, a stranger in a strange land, who seemed to be crying out in protest of what he now saw coming. The hospital called a halt to the surgery.

Someone took him to a small lodging, and after some time, two of Daniel's handlers arrived and began talking among themselves. Daniel understood just enough of what they were saying: they'd take him back to Nigeria, where the kidney could be removed without so much fanfare and red tape.

Before that could happen, Daniel left the flat, wandered the streets of London for two days, slept outdoors for two nights, and finally, near Heathrow Airport, found a police station. After he made his story clear to the attending officers, Daniel was placed in protective custody as the police organized an investigation. Daniel's ordeal led to the UK's first human trafficking prosecution related to organ removal.

At the time of this writing, Daniel is still under police protection, afraid to return home, and missing his family. He no longer wants to live in the UK or anywhere other than home, but it might be dangerous for him to return. Those same criminals prowl the streets.

But the British police have taken note. They're currently busy investigating similar cases. Their finding was that his case was no one-off occurrence. It was part of a trend of people being hustled out of their organs, deceived or forced into surgeries they didn't desire due to the high price and low availability of those parts legally.[11]

Organ trafficking is one more way that human life, and all that constitutes it, is devalued as one more object to place on the open market for the highest bidder.

THE ELUSIVE CRIME

At one time or another, most people have heard the old urban legend about the hapless traveler who is a victim of theft: He is taken to a

---

11. Mark Lobel, Kate West, and Melanie Stewart-Smith, "Organ harvesting: Trafficked for his kidney and now forced into hiding," *BBC*, June 26, 2023, https://www.bbc.com/news/65960515.

hotel room by a beautiful woman, only to be drugged and to wake up in a bathtub filled with ice. He sees quite a bit of blood, locates fresh stitches, and finds out one of his kidneys has been removed.

Urban legends are stories, almost always untrue, that spread wildly because they touch on some deep human fear—in this case the fear of traveling and being among strangers. For years, folklorists assured us this wildly unlikely scenario was a bit of fantasy. But in recent years, it has approached a much more disturbing realism. Occasionally, what happens doesn't look that different from the urban legend.

The organ trade, also known as the "red trade" or the "blood market," is the oddest and most elusive form of human trafficking. After all, sex trafficking and labor trafficking are pretty old. They stretch back into primitive times, when captives taken in battle could become the possessions of their conquerors, forced to either work or provide sexual gratification. Full organ transplantation, however, has only been possible since 1954, when a kidney was donated in a Boston hospital.

Medical practice has grown much more advanced since then. For instance, in 2022, a genetically modified pig's heart functioned in a human being for a few weeks. But as more types of organ transplants have become possible, the demand for organs has risen at a much higher rate than the supply of organs available.

Delay is also a factor, as declining health is often a ticking clock. The National Kidney Foundation tells us that the average wait time for a legal transplant from a deceased donor is three to five years; with a living donor approximately one year or less.[12] . Many of those in need don't have that much time. Obviously, people will pay a great price—and sometimes an illegal one, to save their own lives or the lives of their loved ones. This creates a lucrative market for criminal opportunists. Global Financial Integrity estimates

12. "Kidney Donation," Organs and Tissues for Transplant, Donate Life America, https://donatelife.net/donation/organs/kidney-donation/, accessed April 22, 2024.

that the organ trade makes $840 million to $1.7 billion in illicit profits, annually fueling organized criminals. One estimate is that, with 123,000 people in the world known to need an organ, theoretically you could make $45 million if you harvested every organ in your body.[13] Of course, you wouldn't be around to enjoy any of that money. Realistically, it's difficult to produce consistent figures for the value of any body part—the going rate depends on too many variables—but we know that the most commonly trafficked organ is the kidney, followed by livers and corneas.

This strange new world of organ transplant has created the phenomenon of "transplant tourism," a phrase that refers to people "shopping" across the globe for the best prices or readiest availability of the surgery they require. Transplant tourism has made this form of trafficking a particularly international one. If the United States prohibits organ trade and polices the crime closely, it may be possible to fly to another country where such an operation can occur. However, it should come as no surprise that many patients return home only to experience future complications from sketchy operations overseas.

It's also true that organs are often represented as voluntarily given when, in actuality, they were taken by force. It may not happen to a single individual who wakes up in an ice-filled bathtub, as in the old story—but there have been cases of kidneys and other organs being harvested from people rounded up and held by force. The *Washington Post* reported such an instance. In 2016 in Pakistan, police raided an Islamabad apartment and found twenty-four people locked in a room. They had been gathered through bogus promises or threats, and the next step would have been a trip to a clinic for kidney removal operations.[14]

---

13. Laci Green, "How Much Are Your Body Parts Worth," Seeker, *YouTube*, August 19, 2014, https://www.youtube.com/watch?v=yNOsoe44c40.

14. Asif Efrat, "Organ traffickers lock up people to harvest their kidneys," *The Washington Post*, December 7, 2016, https://www.washingtonpost.com/news/monkey-cage/wp/2016/12/07/organ-traffickers-lock-up-people-to-harvest-their-kidneys-here-are-the-politics-behind-the-organ-trade.

People with difficult lives—refugees, migrants, the poor, and asylum seekers—are targeted. They're offered cash or, like Daniel, some new job that breaks through the daily gloom of their experience. Desperation and hope are some of the best tools for traffickers. And again, there's a tie-in to other forms of the crime. Once the patient heals from the organ removal, that patient may be used for enforced labor or the sex trade.

Nepal is another example. About half the population of 29 million is impoverished. Mount Everest towers over the nation's border with China, and wealthy climbers come from all over the world to scale the notorious peak, only to return home. Meanwhile, 35,000 citizens of this country are sold into slavery. Not long ago, a trafficking network was found that was moving people into India for the purpose of kidney removal. Police closed down a network that was going into the villages and recruiting poor workers, transporting them to New Delhi, drugging them, then taking them to a specific hospital (always the same one) and doing the operation. The victims were (at best) given a small amount of money, then sent home to find their lives damaged forever. They could only do light work. Their energy was limited.[15]

OUR INMOST PARTS

The Bible tells us that God lovingly created our *"inmost being,"* that we are *"fearfully and wonderfully made"* (Psalm 139:13–14). Indeed, we are *"God's handiwork"* (Ephesians 2:10). When we discuss the organs of our body, we are talking about more than blood, bone, and tissue. We're talking about the fine art and perfect craftsmanship of God, the Creator of this world. And surely, if we're made in His image (see Genesis 1:27), then we are indeed His masterpiece.

---

15. Zeba Warsi, "Human trafficking victims forced to sell their organs share harrowing stories," *PBS NewsHour*, January 17, 2023, https://www.pbs.org/newshour/show/human-trafficking-victims-forced-to-sell-their-organs-share-harrowing-stories.

You or I may not feel like a divine masterpiece most of the time. We may not look at others and see a work of art. But all we need to do is think about the wonder, the efficiency, the versatility of the human body, to realize how much we take for granted. This work of flesh and bone may function for up to a century in the wear and tear of this world, self-repairing its daily wounds, creating new skin and cells constantly. Modern science is nowhere close to being capable of creating such a thing, and it never will be.

We think about the mysteries of the human circulatory system and the pumping heart; the digestive system; the networks of smoothly functioning muscles; and above all the crown of every human skull—the brain. The mind can understand in depth many things, but it can't plumb the mysteries of itself. So elusive are the brain's synapses and circuits, its message system, its speed, its amazing filing room of memories, that we can't begin to understand how it smoothly runs the entire operation of being a human being, for decade after decade. As we sleep and refresh, the brain is still at work.

These carbon-based machines are unparalleled to earthly creation. It begins to make sense why we're reminded, in 1 Corinthians, that our bodies are no less than holy temples, in which the Spirit of God comes to dwell. (See 1 Corinthians 6:19.) To the ancient mind, when that verse was written, nothing could be conceived of as more holy, more set apart, than a temple. God will not dwell on a mountain, a star, or in a sunrise. But He will dwell in these temples called humanity.

No matter how modern science seems to present the body as so much organic material, it's special and worthy of reverence—not just the soul but the whole physical package. If you or I had a miniature sculpture created by Michelangelo, we would probably take exceptional care of it. We would consider it utterly precious. We would let no harm come to it. Is the artwork of God any less valuable?

People themselves are God's image bearers. The body is the home God built and furnished, meant to be shared by His Spirit and our own. It is to be treated with utter dignity, never devalued, never seized, never taken by force or deception.

MYTH AND REALITY

It can be hard to believe trafficking of any kind is common in our world. The nightmarish element of somehow being taken prisoner or offered some kind of bait, only to have one's freedom taken away, or perhaps to lose a body part—we want to think humanity has outgrown such primitive evil.

Many of us need a reality check. But we need to make sure that check reflects reality. In this age of social media, information is more freely available than it has ever been. Unfortunately, so is *disinformation*. In the old days, an urban legend such as the tale of the traveler in the bathtub circulated by word of mouth, ear to ear. Now it only needs to be posted on social media. As it's been said, a lie can travel around the world before the truth can rise and put its shoes on. The more shocking a post on Facebook, the more it will be shared, perhaps gaining millions of viewers.

Instead of urban legends spread by mouth, we have disinformation spread over various forms of media, including social media. Those who use social media need to be discerning because mixed in with the truth is a fair amount of inaccuracy and outright falsehood, often designed to collect and influence viewers for an agenda or to claim attention.

Are Hollywood elites kidnapping children, stealing their organs, and drinking their blood? That's just one example of some of the more fantastical and unsourced material floating around. Some people are fooled; others see through it. The real danger is that crucial, solid truth gets lost in a blizzard of propaganda. To some people, sex, labor, and organ trafficking are wholly nonexistent, simply because a few of the stories they read on these topics proved to be ridiculous. If the boy cries wolf enough times, no one will believe him when the real wolf appears.

The challenge is to find out who the truth tellers are, give them our trust, and help them spread their message, while stepping up to expose falsehood whenever we detect it. We need to vet any message before we forward it to others.

Something to think about: it's been said that Satan's greatest accomplishment was to convince people he didn't exist. Could it be that an important goal of traffickers is to spread so many lies about their subject that the truth itself isn't believable after a while?

There's no actual evidence of cartels of Hollywood elites harvesting children's organs or drinking their blood. But there's solid evidence of wide scale forced organ removals in Chinese prison camps, where there are 1.5 million detainees. Investigators have concluded that many prisoners are executed for the organs, feeding a $1 billion transplant trade in that country. In many cases, the victims seem to be targeted and imprisoned for their religious beliefs.

Without truth and accuracy, fighting against trafficking will be a struggle. We need to know more, whether we're in the United States or elsewhere in the world.

Everything begins with truth. Jesus said, *"You shall know the truth, and the truth shall make you free"* (John 8:32 NKJV). Myths only make us confused.

8

LOVE, SEX, AND PREDATORS

Madison can't quite remember how she and Daniel777 became friends, but she thinks TikTok brought them together—actually, she's sure of it.

Most of her Internet friends come from TikTok, the social media app of choice for her and her friends. Madison loves it because it's all about creativity. It's another place to post videos made by smartphones, but she loves how easy the app makes it to add music, speed up or slow down the action, and grab an audience. And everything is fast and loose.

Daniel777 is just one of many friends she met through the comment section. (*That's* how they met; she remembers now—the comment section.) He had some funny snark about her dance moves. After that, she seemed to run into him on other feeds on TikTok—Daniel777, so friendly and quick to leave an outrageous remark.

Their comments led to them messaging back and forth and then texting, which was also fun. He encouraged Madison to keep sharing her talent. He also admitted he thought she was really cute and told her about his school and family. He even shared a picture of himself.

One thing led to another. As they became closer, Daniel777 asked for an intimate photo. Madison was a little uncomfortable about that and said no at first. But Daniel777 said he was really depressed that day. Dark thoughts. He needed something nice, and she meant a lot to him, so could she share a topless picture with him?

Madison considered Daniel777's request. Maybe she could do it, just once. A harmless photo might make a difference for someone thinking dark thoughts. To be honest, she was a little flattered, too. He was intelligent, funny, and good-looking. Nobody like that at school would give her the time of day.

She sent the picture and, later, a few others that he requested. He was so very grateful. He told her she ought to be a model, maybe an actress.

Madison got used to "modeling" for him. She knew she was lucky that her parents never checked her Snapchat or text accounts—she would have hated for them to find out. But really, again, being absolutely honest, the whole thing was kind of sexy. He'd sent her a few hot pictures, too.

Daniel777 didn't seem depressed at this point. Now, he was all about photos—and videos, too. He told her just how to light them and set them up like professionals, and he would ask her to do certain things.

Madison soon became uncomfortable with her arrangement with Daniel777. "No, Dan, babe, we need to quit this thing. It's getting out of hand," she texted.

That was when she saw another side of him—a side that wasn't like her sweet, shy friend. He told her she *was* going to keep on making her movies and she was going to make them *exactly* as he said.

"What?" she texted. "RU JOKING??? NOT FUNNY. Four angry face emojis."

"Absolutely not joking," he replied quickly. "I know a lot about you, your parents, your friends. I would hate to show them all these pictures and videos."

Madison stopped and stared at her phone in shock. Why would Daniel act this way? Then she thought about it a little more, and an awful, unthinkable feeling flooded her thoughts.

"Is your name even Daniel?" she asked.

"LOL of course not. Are u just figuring that out?" he mockingly responded.

Madison turned off her phone, ran to the bathroom, and vomited. She couldn't think of what to do. Could she change her number? That wouldn't work. Dad would ask questions. Besides, there was nowhere to hide. Daniel777, whoever and wherever he really was, knew *everything* about her life.

Call the police? Absolutely not. For one thing, that would mean telling her parents the whole story. Also, she was smart enough to know that the police would never find this predator. He could be anywhere in the world. She knew almost nothing about him besides a few fake pictures and stories. He had covered his tracks.

She didn't turn her phone on for three days, making excuses to her parents. But sooner or later, she had to do it, and she knew the horrors that would be waiting for her there. She was now providing a steady stream of pedophilic pornography, most of it disgusting, and there was no escape.

Only a short time after that, Madison received a message demanding her to come to a specific address, within bicycle distance of her home. "Send more videos now or pay us $5,000. If you tell *anyone at all*, people you love will be hurt and all your pictures go online. Come eager and ready to star in some new films, and to be cooperative. Or else."

Madison was the latest victim of what is now being called "sextortion"—extortion using sexual information via text message.

THE LOVE CONNECTION

Everyone needs to give and receive love. It's such a powerful drive that it makes some of us predictable. It becomes one of the easiest buttons for others to push if they want to exploit us.

In the modern world, we spend a great deal of time watching movies, following TV shows, and reading books about love, romance, and happy endings. It's no coincidence that this is the number one subject in our stories and fantasies. We imagine ourselves in the roles played before us, finding perfect love with a perfect partner for a perfect future together.

But it's more than old-fashioned, boy-meets-girl romance. Sex is a factor, too. More today than in any other era, we live in a sex-saturated society. As if sex doesn't cross the human mind enough already, our media ensures that we think about it even more by using sex to sell products and command attention.

The result is a generation with warped, confused ideas about this subject. Celebrities (our generation's set of heroes) are looked upon as sex objects. Pornography is a billion-dollar industry, recession-proof and continuing to grow and find new outlets.

It's no wonder so many young people are struggling today, during the period of their lives when they depart from childhood and test their identities as sexual creatures for the first time. During a period when they come to grips with group identity, popularity, and the frightening new world of dating, the idea of sex looms over everything far more than in previous periods of history.

The predator takes advantage of this emotionally charged situation by using the tools of technology to appear under a false, unthreatening identity, and manipulate naïve children. They know how to gain trust and abuse it.

Sextortion is one way of manipulating teens that can lead to unintended participation in pornography. From there, it could potentially lead even to being trapped in a sex trafficking ring. Whatever the direction, a young person is caught in a cycle of shame and exploitation with no easy way out.

In one case, the victim—we'll call him "Jeremy"—met a love interest online, sent compromising pictures of himself, and was threatened when he made it clear he wanted to stop. It turned out that the "love interest" was a group of three Nigerian men; in this case, the men demanded money. Jeremy was faced with the choice of producing a financial ransom or being exposed before the world online. In a panic, Jeremy did what too many young people are now doing: he took his own life. And then—and this should give us some idea of the depth of evil involved—on the first anniversary of Jeremy's death, the criminals contacted his parents on social media merely to gloat.

As much as we've stressed that money is the ultimate goal of all these crimes, we must recognize there is a deep level of evil involved as well—an evil that glories in destroying human beings.

Children's love of video games opens another door for predators to slip through. Kids make new friends through online gaming all the time, without knowing who these people are in real life. The criminals don't care whether they're working through social media, gaming, or other venues. Their goal is to entrap new victims.

The fact that children and young teens are targeted is particularly difficult for us to fathom. Unfortunately, there's a high market value for younger boys and girls, and they have to be procured somewhere. In the old days, perhaps predators would lurk at the local bus station of a big city and entice teenage runaways. The Internet has made it much, much easier than that.

TOOLS FOR COMBAT

As we've seen this particularly heinous trend emerge, we at Dark Watch have begun to devote more time to working with parents and schools to educate them on what's happening online and equip them with the tools to help children stay safe in cyberspace. As of 2016, 95 percent of our children aged eighteen or younger—twenty-four out of twenty-five—had home Internet access.[16] The potential harvest couldn't be greater for predators.

During the past generation, we've done a good job of teaching our children about "stranger danger." They know not to take candy from the guy in the van. Now, we need to teach a slightly tougher message: strangers are online, too, and they're much harder to recognize. They may claim to be your age, and they may *seem* to prove it. But we must be exceedingly careful in this strange terrain known as the Internet. Can parents get that message across? Can they monitor their children's actions online, even as their teenage children push back and demand privacy?

Parents and guidance counselors are the first line of defense in sextortion, so we've helped them build a toolset to respond effectively. It involves a five-step framework to begin the discussion:

1. **Talk to your children clearly and openly.** Tell them about the danger, show them that sextortion is an actual and active trend, and not just a theoretical idea, and give them real-life examples, such as the ones in this chapter.

2. **Provide a safe environment to discuss online activities and problems.** As a more general parenting practice (and this applies in schools as well), strive to create an

---

16. "Internet Access from Home," Fast Facts: Access to the Internet, National Center for Education Statistics, https://nces.ed.gov/fastfacts/display.asp?id=46#fn1.

open environment in which children and teenagers can share what's happening in their lives. Listen and express care and compassion without immediately giving guidance.

3. **Check privacy settings and content sharing on social media sites.** Administrator settings on our home networks and computers allow us to control what can be shared and how. Parents or guardians need to know what Internet-connected devices are being used and ensure the settings protect their children.

4. **Stay informed about how kids use gaming, social media, and dating platforms.** It's easy for tech-talk from a younger generation to become so much white noise for parents. We hear about online games, new social media sites, and various terms, and we may not understand the references. As responsible parents, we must make the effort to understand some of the fine details of our children's worlds. The less we understand, the less safety we're capable of providing.

5. **Contact the police if you suspect sextortion, human trafficking, or any other serious criminal activity.** Some parents hesitate because they're reluctant to accept the terrifying possibility that something terrible may have happened. Err on the side of caution. If nothing dangerous is going on, officers of the law will help to ease our minds. If there is, in fact, danger, we need their help immediately.

Predators are shifty, so it takes extra vigilance to detect their presence. For example, a criminal will set up a fake account with a nice picture and send friend requests to all the students at a middle school. If only five or ten respond, that's all that's necessary. The predator has a bank of "friends in common" to work from when reaching out to others. "I don't know this person, but he knows three of my friends, so I guess he's okay." The scammer will then focus on one individual who seems lonely and vulnerable.

It's impossible to overemphasize how cautious our children should be on social media. In this case, parents and children shouldn't accept requests from strangers. If they do seem to know a few of our friends, we should first ask those friends how they know them; it may turn out they don't know them at all.

Dark Watch stands ready to assist any family, school, or church that might benefit from training on sextortion and online safety. You can contact me at noel@darkwatch.io or our website at https://darkwatch.io.

Training and communication are the best tools we have to guard against danger. Don't wait until there's a tragedy in your neighborhood, school, or home. A scheduled training session may save the unthinkable from occurring in your community.

PIG BUTCHERING

Sha Zhu Pan. In Chinese, it means, quite literally, "pig butchering." Pig butchering is a scam originating in China where scammers manipulate victims to obtain their funds. The idea of butchering a pig is that we fatten the pig and then feast. But the fattening can be through finance or romance. Either can lead to sex trafficking.

In 2022, Netflix presented a true crime documentary called *The Tinder Swindler.* It related the cautionary tale of a con man named Simon Leviev, who scammed people out of at least ten million dollars through the social media app Tinder. He met women online, took them on expensive dates to the finest restaurants (sometimes on private jets), and swept them off their feet. Then, he told them he desperately needed to borrow money to fight his "enemies." He sent all the women a picture that seemed to offer evidence he had suffered a knife attack, only to be rescued by his bodyguard. His told them that his security had been breached, and he couldn't use any of his credit cards. He had to have money now or he would lose something of value. Leviev would use the money that poured in from the women to invest in wooing other women, and the cycle would continue. Later, he would pretend to pay back the money, would delay, would threaten the women, then eventually break off the relationship.

This was a gilded variation on sextortion, designed for adult women and with more of a financial angle.

In a great many pig butchering cases, cryptocurrency is used. It's a form of cash transfer that can't be traced, so it's ideal for online scam artists. The victims often know little or nothing about cryptocurrency, and the criminals promise to talk them through it, making deposits in their own name, which seems safe enough.

As we saw in Madison's story at the beginning of the chapter, predators can find a small crack in the wall—a tiny opening in someone's defenses. From there, the predator can build what seems like a deep and trusting relationship. The pig is being fattened for the kill. In Madison's case, the crack in her defenses was her good sense of humor and willingness to accept encouragement.

We may be tempted to write off this issue as something that affects only the naïve—someone dumb enough to fall for it. Consider this, though: the Tinder Swindler picked up his dates in person, on a personal jet. Who could blame these women for falling for his deception? It's even easier to mislead teens and preteens on a social media app. The predator may be in another country and may be sixty years old, but in the victim's imagination, he's a nice boy from a good family who lives a few states away and enjoys the same bands.

Pig butchering, with the goal of some form of trafficking or financial theft, is becoming big business. The Justice Department seized over $112 million related to one pig butchering scheme. No jet planes were used, but the con artists had created fake websites and even mobile apps that seemed to show their investors accumulating money. The investors would then enthusiastically send more money through cryptocurrency. It was a get-rich-quick scheme that seemed all too real. Sadly, all that money was headed for the pockets of a criminal ring. Eventually, in this case, the six bank accounts containing the proceeds were seized by a judge's order.[17]

Sadly, the criminal groups behind this type of fraud are rarely caught. They could be operating from anywhere in the world, and they go to great lengths to leave no fingerprints. In the case of trafficking, it often turns out the perpetrators are individuals who have been trafficked. It's part of their slavery—being the "cut outs" on the front line of a scheme, so that if anyone takes the fall, it's another victim rather than the criminal.

LOGGING OFF AND LIVING BETTER

The Internet is regarded as one of the most impactful human inventions of the last thousand years. It's an amazing network connecting people from every corner of the earth, providing information, entertainment, and even spiritual ministry. During the COVID-19 pandemic, the Internet enabled hundreds of millions of people to worship together, see their friends' faces, and keep their prayer and Bible study groups going without ever leaving their homes. Businesses learned to operate over video connections.

The Internet can be good. But it can also be the valley of the shadow of death. (See Psalm 23:4.) Some of the most dangerous and evil ideas humanity has concocted are available there. It offers the temptation of pornography. It sends evil messages to our children that can drown out what their parents teach them. The

---

17. Press Release, "Justice Dept. Seizes Over $112M in Funds Linked to Cryptocurrency Investment Schemes, With Over Half Seized in Los Angeles Case," United States Attorney's Office Central District of California, April 3, 2023, https://www.justice.gov/usao-cdca/pr/justice-dept-seizes-over-112m-funds-linked-cryptocurrency-investment-schemes-over-half.

possibility of unthinkable tragedy lurks amid the fun and fellow-ship designed by social media companies.

The Internet is like money—neither good nor evil, but capable of being used for either. We need to guide our children in how they use it. There is software available that filters out unwanted influences. But nothing works as well as attentive, loving parenting. Our children don't want to fall into the hands of online predators. They must know what dangers are present, and how to avoid them.

Usage limits must be set and carefully explained. Phones, apps, and video games need not be so all-consuming. Try exercising electronic fasting within the family once a week, so no one forgets what real, face-to-face living is about. We all need to unplug occasionally, get off the grid, and spend a little of that time reacquainting ourselves with each other and our Creator, with whom we can chat anytime at all—without clicks, typing, emoticons, or the fear of deception.

9

ORGANIZED RETAIL CRIME AND HUMAN TRAFFICKING

Aubrey Plaza received excellent reviews for her 2022 film *Emily the Criminal*. In the movie, she plays the title character, a twenty-something young lady down on her luck. Emily made a bad decision in her past, which led to an arrest after a violent episode. A chain reaction of events kept her from obtaining the kind of job her education prepared her for. The one job she was able to land as a delivery driver for a catering service didn't compensate her enough to pay off her college loans. Emily needed cash.

A friend from work gave her a phone number, which led Emily to a "dummy shopper" service. She was curious what that might be. "How would you like to make two hundred bucks in one hour?" asked the director of the service. Emily received a fake ID and credit card. They were convincing enough to allow her to leave a store with her purchase.

Emily was then taken to a big-box appliance retailer, where her job was to buy a top-of-the-line flat-screen TV with the credit card and get out before her credentials gave out. Outside, she handed the TV to a team member, who packed it into his van. She was handed ten crisp twenty-dollar bills, and the van whisked her away. It was the easiest money she'd ever made.

The leader then asked her, "How'd you like to make a bigger score than that one?" The next day, she was sent to purchase a high-end luxury car. This time, the scam failed, and she narrowly escaped arrest and a significant prison sentence.

Emily's situation isn't just the work of an imaginative screenwriter. It's an example of *organized retail crime* (ORC), which has created a lot of momentum in the shopping world. In the movie, Emily would never have committed the crime, with its high-risk factor, unless she were genuinely desperate. She opted in because she was drowning in loan debt. In real life, actors like Aubrey Plaza aren't working the scam; many times, it's individuals caught in trafficking. It's shoplifting on a large, expensive, and more complex scale, carried out by organized crime organizations.

Retail trade and lobby groups estimate that theft accounts for 65–70 percent of shrinkage ("measurement of losses calculated by a retailer during a specific period of time"). Shrinkage represented $112.1 billion in 2022.[18]

It happens quickly, during peak hours in a busy store, and the perpetrators, known as "boosters," are hard to catch because they get in and out quickly—and are helped by professional thieves. They might bring a detailed list of items to buy, as those who supervise them know exactly what the market wants at any given time. The merchandise is sold to fences, who pay in cash or perhaps drugs. Then, it's sent to market in discount stores or online auctions. The thieves might even sell the goods back to retailers, who remove ID numbers and get a "deal" from the fences. That special "damaged box" deal may

---

18. "Organized Retail Crime," Policy Issues, National Retail Federation, accessed April 23, 2024, https://nrf.com/advocacy/policy-issues/organized-retail-crime.

have already made the rounds, only to return to the store from where it was stolen.

Some boosters are like Emily in the movie—either hard up for cash, or simply looking for a quick and easy way to a big payday, regardless of whether that involves theft. However, trafficked individuals can also be forced into this line of work. It's always the boosters who run the highest risk. If they don't emerge from the store with the merchandise within a reasonable amount of time, the van hits the road, abandoning the boosters to face the consequences.

Even if trafficking isn't involved in the actual theft, ORC schemes are often used to bankroll human trafficking operations. ORC produces fast money, quick and untraceable, at low risk. Proceeds are laundered through the financial world through traditional money laundering practices. Boosters move from city to city, so they'll be more challenging to identify and can hit fresh retail targets.

Organized crime has created plenty of other angles, too— stolen gift cards or gift card balances, for example. Gift cards are easy and popular gifts, but they lack the security features an ordinary credit card has, and there are many ways scammers can translate them into capital and then use them in retail theft. If someone wants to pay you in gift cards, that's a flashing warning light. Telephone or email scammers try to deceive people into buying certain kinds of gift cards and then giving them the serial numbers off the cards, which are as good as money. It's even possible the caller is being trafficked.

This brings crime into the world of data and the Internet, and it creates an opportunity for Dark Watch to work with retailers to trace some of the information that will help identify the criminals. As always, the digital element creates opportunities for crime but can also furnish a trail back to the criminal.

THE TRAFFICKING CONNECTION

Quite often trafficking stories begin with immigrants trying to cross the border into the United States. As there's been much more attention given to border security recently, with greater surveillance, border crossers have been forced to hire "coyotes," individuals who transport them across the border, through security, and into the United States. When legislation was passed in 1996 to tighten up on assisting in illegal crossings, the coyotes weren't deterred—they just increased their fees. Now coyote work is a multibillion-dollar industry.

Once the immigrants are in Texas, Arizona, or California, they owe their transporter a fee. A great number of the immigrants cannot pay, as they have left everything behind in their former homes. This is when labor trafficking and sex trafficking often begin. The coyotes know these refugees are helpless. Retail theft rings are just one option of where the coyotes can deliver their human cargo. And even if the coyote doesn't push them down this route, the immigrants still find they have few options for finding work in the United States. So they're easy targets for traffickers. They're also more likely to fall under suspicion when they are shopping for expensive items, and if they fail and are apprehended, they're simply deported while the trafficker simply finds new boosters.

My friend Tom worked to stop organized retail theft. In one store, as he patrolled the aisles and observed, his eyes fell upon a man who, at first glance, seemed to be impoverished. His hair and complexion weren't well cared for, and he wore clothing that had seen better days. Oddly enough, however, he was wearing luxury loafers, and an expensive watch gleamed from his wrist. Keeping his distance, Tom monitored the man's movements inside and outside the store, and he ultimately identified the man as part of an organized human trafficking group being used for theft. In this case, the inconsistency in the man's looks brought scrutiny.

It can be difficult to detect those who are part of organized retail theft. General health and hygienic indicators can sometimes identify people being trafficked in this way; in general, these people aren't well cared for and possibly don't care much about their appearance. General demeanor can also be an indicator. They'll seem frightened, shy away from interaction, or perhaps seem eager to immediately leave if approached. Sometimes, they'll be accompanied by someone else who seems to hold authority over them and who steps in to intercede. Thus, trafficking victims and coerced theft participants may not give themselves away by wearing a Rolex, but the evidence will be in their demeanor: nervousness, fear, anxiety, and timidity. There may be signs of abusive treatment and confinement.

Experienced shoplifters will be more difficult to identify than unwilling participants in a theft ring, who stand out from typical, casual shoppers. It's just a matter of watching carefully and teaching others to do the same.

In raising awareness of how to identify participants of organized retail theft, we must remember that it's not just a matter of preventing the store from incurring a financial loss, but of saving people who are being used and discarded by traffickers. With this goal in mind, we offer training for retailers, who find our presentations very helpful and practical. Hundreds of shoppers or more may flood through a store during the day. Those working in the store may stop paying much attention to what the shoppers look like. But a little attentiveness can prevent a crime and perhaps even save a life.

It's good for all of us, in whatever our occupation, to pay attention to those around us. For instance, consider the case of Shelia Fredrick. She was a well-trained flight attendant who was careful to keep her eyes open. In 2017, she spotted a teenage girl while on a flight from Seattle to San Francisco. Flight passengers come from every sector of society, but this girl looked utterly miserable and desperate. Her clothing was in disarray, and her blonde hair appeared not to have been washed in weeks. Her companion was a very well-to-do older man. The pair made an odd couple, to put it mildly.

Fedrick engaged the two in conversation. She found that the girl was basically unresponsive, always looking to the man for direction. He, on the other hand, was defensive and not eager to chat. Fedrick suggested to the girl that she might want to use the restroom, where she left a note and a pen so the girl could respond. She included her personal phone number and an invitation to call if she needed assistance.

I need help, the girl wrote in response.

Fedrick informed the pilot about her interaction with the couple, and when the plane touched down in San Francisco, the authorities were waiting for the man. He was found to be a human trafficker.

All of this was possible because of a group called Airline Ambassadors, which trains flight staff in detecting the signs of human trafficking.[19] It's an example of how we can consider which businesses might encounter this issue and recognize that criminals will turn up at certain times and in certain places. For instance, before a big sporting event such as the Super Bowl, sex traffickers will be drawn to the location of the game and the major hotels near it. Can hotel employees be on the lookout? What about local restaurant staff? We need well-trained employees at retail stores and other hot spots who understand that "if you see something, say something."

NEW CHALLENGES

Organized retail crime continues to grow, even with the attention it's receiving. Human trafficking is a nexus crime, connected to so

19. Kalhan Rosenblatt, "Flight Attendants Train to Spot Human Trafficking," *NBC News*, February 4, 2017, https://www.nbcnews.com/storyline/airplane-mode/flight-attendants-train-spot-human-trafficking-n716181.

many others; we need to address both problems because the crises don't simply go away—they grow much worse.

Organized retail crime is a much more dangerous and sophisticated variation of shoplifting, which was already a well-established problem. ORC is costing retailers billions of dollars, while ramping up the need for more people to be forced into trafficking so they can do the heavy lifting. But as stores grow more resistant and beef up their security, new attacks appear—for example, "flash mobs." In a flash mob, many boosters arrive at a prearranged time to overwhelm security. Violence in stores is also becoming a bigger problem.

Retailers are using technology and training to stop their inventory from vanishing off the shelves without being paid for. They're also lobbying for stricter laws to fight organized retail crime. One proposed act will require online sites to verify the identities of those using their marketplaces for high-volume third-party sellers. If you buy those Bluetooth headphones at a reduced price from an independent seller on eBay or Amazon, that seller will have to have been vetted very carefully.

Other government acts would provide resources to make their stores more theft-proof. The largest retailers are meeting to exchange ideas and discuss ways technology and training can increase the security in their stores.

We hope they succeed. Think about the retailers and wholesalers who lose money; that's not good for the economy. Think about the criminal organizations driving these illegal enterprises—they shouldn't even exist.

We also need to think about the real victims. In the middle of this phenomenon is the individual with the greatest risk. It could be an impoverished villager from Guatemala who was trying to find a better life and was scooped up at the border to be loaded into a truck and used for all kinds of forced labor, theft, and other activities. It could be a runaway teenage girl who fought with her parents, hopped on a bus in an impulsive moment, and soon—out of money and food—fell into a human trafficking ring in which she is sold from market to market, and from dangerous encounter to dangerous encounter. It could be a young man who wasn't hirable in a respectable job for one reason or another. He took a gig boosting certain pharmaceuticals from drug stores, with absolutely no intention of doing it in the future. He was in urgent need of cash to get by, and now he's being blackmailed and trafficked in a theft ring.

These are all human beings who deserve a better life. God created them to be free, not to be someone else's property. As Jesus promised to set the captives free (see Luke 4:18), it's our task to carry on His work wherever we find captives. They could be in the electronics aisle at the big box store, or in the seat across the aisle on our red-eye flight. These people are around us every day. Do we see them? Can we help them?

10

CRYPTOCURRENCY AND LAUNDERING

The Internal Revenue Service is highly motivated to follow money through criminal channels. Money laundering is one of their primary areas of investigation.

Chris Janczewski formerly served as a special agent with the Internal Revenue Service's criminal investigations division. His career had never crossed paths with child sexual abuse; he figured other government agencies were handling those crimes. During his time at the IRS, he found out he was wrong. Neither the FBI nor Homeland Security paid attention to the abuses he encountered in 2017.

Janczewski received information that he should investigate a South Korean website on the dark web. This website required users to pay for access to a vast archive of videos depicting the rape and sexual assault of small children, sometimes babies. But the site wanted payment in Bitcoin. For two years, Janczewski focused on what came to be considered the largest dark web child pornography website in the world. Working with other government agencies and the South Korean police, Janczewski's team had to learn about Bitcoin and then trace thousands of Bitcoin addresses. This led to the arrest of 340 men in 38 countries. At least 25 children were rescued from ongoing child abuse.[20]

To understand cryptocurrency, we should begin with a fundamental review of how money works. Money exists because people need to make trades to help each other: perhaps one person has grown potatoes, and another has a nice bushel of corn; they barter back and forth and eventually make a trade so both of them have some of each. In this situation, the currency is food. But in reality, it's whatever we trade: a thing of value exchanged for something else of value.

In the ancient world, cattle was a common currency. However, not everyone owned cattle. People needed more practical forms of exchange, and there needed to be standards agreed upon. So coins made of valuable metal and notes made of paper were eventually developed as currency. Coins of gold and silver had intrinsic value, but the notes, or bills, were merely symbols that signified a given value of wealth in a bank somewhere. People began calling this currency *money*. The notes were still just paper; they only had value in a world where we all agreed on their worth. We needed this paper because we couldn't carry cows or all our gold in our pockets.

In time, money became more of an idea than a physical item. You may be worth a million dollars, but that doesn't mean you have the actual currency in your bank. Today, sums of capital exchange hands without any physical form of wealth ever entering the picture.

But if wealth is an idea, a mutual agreement, that makes it fragile; it's a measure of confidence, and confidence rises and falls. For instance, if I'm the CEO of a publicly traded company, my company has a value, and it's reflected in my stock price. If a terrible flaw is discovered in our product, public confidence shatters,

20. Corinne Redfern and Seulki Lee, "Sex Criminals Use Bitcoin. So Do the Police," *Foreign Policy*, January 30, 2021, https://foreignpolicy.com/2021/01/30/sex-criminals-use-bitcoin-so-do-the-police.

and stocks plunge. Suddenly, the company isn't worth twenty million; it's worth ten million—maybe less.

It can happen on a national or a global basis. When the financial crisis of 2007 hit, $700 billion *instantly* vanished from retirement plans and other investment funds. Where did it go? Wherever the confidence went. Several factors came together in a perfect storm to create panic in the financial sector, massive withdrawals, and devaluation of capital, and suddenly, there was much less wealth in the world's banks. Lifelong wealth evaporated.

Now comes the world of cryptocurrency, which makes financial realities even more abstract. For one thing, it was designed to be used digitally through a computer network to make financial transactions quickly without a buyer and seller even sharing the same location. But traditional money also does that. We buy through computer networks every day. So what truly distinguishes cryptocurrency?

Bitcoin, the leading form of cryptocurrency, uses a public, permanent, and *decentralized* ledger. The word decentralized is the key. It bears no relationship to any government. It's money that declares independence from all the old rules. For example, say you and I gain a certain amount of wealth in a given year. The government keeps tabs on it, and we pay taxes on it. Cryptocurrency, however, uses *cryptography*, which is a form of hiding information through codes that allows people to use a perfectly viable form of money outside of that centralized authority. The financial system and the government would reply, "You can't do that! No matter what form your wealth takes, it must be reported, must follow the rules, and is liable to taxation." This isn't the case for cryptocurrency.

MONEY-MINING

When people invest in cryptocurrency, not only can they furtively move large or small amounts of money with no fear of it being traced (and taxed), but they can also hope for a particular cryptocurrency, such as Bitcoin (the most valuable crypto), to rise in value, just as other investments might. If, say, the US dollar wasn't performing well in international markets and its value was decreasing, then Bitcoin might be looked upon as a better investment. Bitcoin payments would actually be more desirable than dollar-based payments in certain quarters. If this were happening on a large scale, demand for Bitcoin would increase, and it would have an even higher value. This has happened over the years, particularly as Bitcoin has become fashionable.

Enthusiasts use large networks of computers with high processing power to "mine" Bitcoin. This is how wealth, measured in "Bitcoins," is created. The powerful computers are given highly complex mathematical problems to solve, and as they solve them, perhaps working together with other miners, they are awarded Bitcoins. Users are proving they've earned the financial reward by having the processing power to solve an incredibly obscure equation. They might also verify the authenticity of others' transactions for a reward.

Enthusiasts leave their computers running indefinitely to mine cryptocurrency and make a profit over time. Others, more interested in the "crypto" than the "currency," might purchase Bitcoin with traditional money. Then, they can use it to buy and sell things that might be illegal.

The permanent ledger mentioned above is known as *blockchain*, a durable, tamper-resistant record of transactions and cryptocurrency ownership. Mining creates new pages for the ever-growing blockchain. The ledger is all-important because it provides consistency for the system that holds everything together. It keeps people from cheating the system by copying their own Bitcoin and spending it twice.

That's a fundamental overview of Bitcoin, the earliest and most important form of cryptocurrency. (Don't worry—there won't be a test.) Those of us resisting the growth of organized crime need to be informed about all the tools criminals use, and cryptocurrency has become an important one.

The popularity of and confidence in something as relatively new as Bitcoin has been a roller-coaster ride, but definitely in the direction of growth. In early 2020, the value hovered around ten thousand dollars per bitcoin[21]. But by late 2021, it had reached nearly seventy thousand dollars per bitcoin—700 percent growth in less than two years—all the while surging, plummeting, surging again. The timing should tell you this was an obsession of choice during the height of the COVID-19 pandemic. At the writing of this book, one bitcoin is valued at just over sixty-two thousand dollars.

This unique financial system isn't going anywhere for two principal reasons: first, people love mining for money, and second, the secrecy that is possible. Enthusiasts will tell you it's a purer and more efficient way to handle money than the US dollar or any other national currency. International exchange is much simpler, since crypto knows no borders.

It seems to be the wave of the future, but it's also quite attractive to organized crime because it's far more difficult to monitor than traditional currency.

DIRTY LAUNDRY

Dark Watch's mantra in understanding organized crime is "follow the money." That's the key to exposing nearly any crime—and, usually, it is the reason evil things are done: simple financial gain.

But following the money isn't often straightforward. If those on the side of justice attempt to follow the green trail, those on the criminal side do everything they can to obscure it.

---

21. Bitcoin is a digital currency created for use in peer-to-peer online transactions; bitcoin is a unit of this currency. Merriam-Webster.com Dictionary, s.v. "Bitcoin," accessed April 26, 2024, https://www.merriam-webster.com/dictionary/Bitcoin.

Money laundering is a classic example. It's the attempt to conceal the illegal source of money by converting it into a legal source. Criminals may use a shell corporation and pump cash through it, thus concealing where the money came from. Or a piece of property is purchased in cash for much more than the property is worth. Restaurants and massage parlors can claim many cash payments to launder dirty money. *Smurfing*, also known as structuring, is a method of breaking up a large transaction—one that would register as "suspicious activity"—into several small transactions. Cryptocurrency is ideal for this, and traffickers certainly use these strategies. They also use casinos and hold offshore accounts in tax havens (with loose financial accountability). We've even seen traffickers resort to buying a bank somewhere with weak money laundering controls; this allows them to quickly move money in and out.

Banks and financial institutions are responsible for upholding the anti-money-laundering statutes that safeguard our financial systems. When a bank notices "suspicious activities," such as a very large transaction coming through its channels, it's required to report this to the government. The US Treasury becomes involved if money laundering seems like a possibility. The depositors may have to answer some very sensitive questions, including where the money came from.

As the world changes, these laws and practices must also change. The terrorist attacks on September 11, 2001, plunged the world into an age of terrorism and a war against it. Accounts were sometimes seized to keep money from flowing through to known terroristic organizations.

Money laundering has three elements: placement, layering, and integration or extraction.

+ **Placement:** This is how money launderers introduce money into traditional financial institutions. We've mentioned how shell companies and small businesses can be used to launder money. A cash-heavy business such as a carwash or a diner would help obscure the source of a lot of finance.

+ **Layering:** Cryptocurrency is more likely to come into play here. The complexity of transactions is what counts in layering. We've spoken primarily of Bitcoin, but remember, that's one of thousands of cryptocurrencies. A *mixer* or tumbler is a professional who buys an assortment of cryptocurrencies with other cryptocurrencies so that there are "layers" of cash flow in one large transaction.

+ **Integration:** This completes the phase of moving money around in the laundering process to make it appear legal. When the proceeds are integrated, they have the full appearance of legitimacy. By the time the funds are extracted, their source is untraceable, whether it was drug-dealing or selling people into slavery.

Trillions of dollars might move through laundering processes annually, and hiding it is so vital to criminals that they're willing to accept up to 50 percent of the loss of their gross proceeds to keep the laundering going smoothly. Some Bitcoin ATMs or kiosks work just like ordinary bank ATM machines. The user decides how much money to invest in Bitcoin, gives the machine a QR code or "wallet address," and completes the transaction. Often, Bitcoin ATMs use an exchange rate that can range from 10 to 25 percent, but it can be worth it. Some people may approach the ATM with a duffle bag full of cash, ready to send across borders. Cryptocurrency makes that possible.

PANDORA'S BOX

The ancient Greeks told creative stories to explain the mysteries of the world. How did trouble first enter the universe? In their mythology, a woman named Pandora was given a special box by Zeus, the most powerful of the mythic gods. She was instructed never to open it. Human curiosity is inevitable, however. As soon as Zeus was gone, Pandora lifted the lid to the box, and all the world's troubles escaped in the form of hideous serpents rushing forward to plague the earth. Once these troubles were out of the box, they could never be stuffed back in.

We've "opened the box" on some incredibly powerful technology during our generation, but we had no idea how much evil could result from it. Every smartphone and every form of computer is a box that holds great danger for the world. Since we'll never close the lid, we must be much smarter about tracking down all the evil forces bringing suffering to our world through technology.

Traffickers use cryptocurrency not only to transact but to launder their profits. It's no longer as simple to follow the path of the money as it was when we were using the Backpage website as a kind of GPS pointing to traffickers. Marketplaces on the dark web don't accept forms of currency other than cryptocurrency. Buyers can easily purchase fentanyl and various synthetic opioids on these seedy alleys of the Internet. Trafficking is growing, but measuring this growth is getting much more difficult as the money trails go cold.

There is one final element to the story of Pandora's box that is often forgotten. After all the troubles had escaped, only one thing was left behind. It went by the name of Hope. For centuries, people have argued over why such a wonderful thing would have been found within a box holding so many evil things. Maybe the question is the whole point: hope isn't based on reason but faith. It stands firm when everything seems bleak. It sees its way to something better.

We can be encouraged because *"hope does not put us to shame, because God's love has been poured out into our hearts through the Holy Spirit, who has been given to us"* (Romans 5:5). In that love, we will continue to fight human trafficking.

But how, exactly? Once again, data comes to the rescue—or at least gives us hope. He who lives by virtual currency dies by virtual currency. The process of trading crypto obscures users, but with Bitcoin, at least, there's the blockchain. That's the permanent ledger that governs all Bitcoin transactions. It's unchangeable, but it's also public and transparent. Even if we can't see who is moving money, we can still track its movements through blockchain.

Chainalysis is a company based in New York City dedicated to studying blockchain and deciphering its path to the criminal element. Chainalysis Reactor is software that helps with that task. Government agencies used it with great success in the Welcome to Video takedown of the largest child pornography website in the world. Chainalysis Reactor played an important role. It was also involved in the notorious Silk Road marketplace shutdown, which recovered more than one billion dollars of criminally collected money.

We must use all the weapons in our armory. That means investigating on the ground, breaking up massage parlors used for prostitution and trafficking; it means being as deft with crypto-currency as the criminals are; and it means being persistent and vigilant, ready to fight back until there is truly zero trafficking. We're dug in for the duration and continuing to develop new weapons. We pray that a generation of gifted young people will enlist and join us in the trenches.

11

TRAFFICKING IN THE DARK— AND IN THE CLEAR

We think of the Internet as an open, welcoming place—even a community. It renders the world as a neighborhood where you can zip between distant sites in the blink of an eye. Its staggering size never intimidates us because we spend most of our time at familiar stops—shopping on Amazon, engaging on Facebook, and reading and responding to email. But do we have a sense of how enormous the realm of cyberspace has grown and continues to grow?

Those who have been around a few decades remember when the roads and signage in the virtual landscape weren't so clear. In the mid-nineties, when the World Wide Web was new, the Internet was famously described as a nearly infinite library holding all the books in the world—but the pages were scattered randomly across the floor.[22] The information you wanted was out there, but, pre-Google wizardry, it was exceedingly difficult to find.

That was then, and this is now. Most of us can get around, and children are growing up with standard Internet savvy.

---

22. Jonathan Salem Baskin, *Histories of Social Media* (Shadows on the Cave Wall: Glencoe, IL, 2011), 103.

However, the dangers have increased along with the conveniences, and they have increased equally on the Internet's hidden dark web and on sites easily accessible to any computer that doesn't use filters.

Serena K. Fleites's ordeal testifies to those dangers.[23] Serena was a student earning top grades in Bakersfield, California. She'd never been kissed, but she developed a crush on a young man who seemed to share her feelings. Then he asked her to text him an explicit video of herself. Serena refused, but the young man kept pressuring her. Finally he threatened to break up with her unless she came through with some explicit footage. Serena gave into the pressure, but one video didn't satisfy him. He continued to ask. Serena had to admit it made her feel attractive and desirable to have someone so fascinated by her body.

But one day, kids at school began acting odd around her—staring and whispering. It turns out, her boyfriend had shared the videos she'd sent him, and one of the recipients uploaded them to a site called Pornhub, a website filled with sexually explicit videos. Serena's was labeled, "Thirteen-year-old brunette shows off for the camera."

That was the end of ordinary life as Serena had known it. She was only fourteen. Now she was labeled with profane language. Some boys approached her wanting videos of their own; they threatened to show Serena's mother what was going on if she didn't send them. The school suspended Serena's boyfriend, but that only added fuel to the fire. Serena, posing as her mother (who had yet to find out), begged Pornhub to take down the videos—but they would always be re-uploaded. Pornhub allows downloading, so people could keep copies and continue using them.

Serena changed schools, but the rumors eventually caught up with her. She began cutting herself, and she attempted suicide

---

23. *Fleites v. MindGeek S.A.R.L.*, 2:21-CV-04920-CJC-ADS (C.D. Cal. Oct. 14, 2022), https://casetext.com/case/fleites-v-mindgeek-sarl.

twice: with pills and then by hanging. But each time, she was revived. In time, Serena became addicted to meth and opioids, which offered her relief from despair. She left home and, finally, having no access to money, returned to taking pictures of herself. She was living in her car when she told an interviewer she was working to get her life back—maybe even go back to school and train for a career.

Serena spoke of "one little mistake" that devastated her life. The question is whether such a mistake and its consequences should have so much power. Unfortunately, that's the state of play these days. We've built an Internet capable of both sublime miracles and soulless abomination.[24]

ON THE DARK SIDE

The Internet, indeed, has a nefarious side of town. But maybe that's the wrong metaphor. It can't be a "side of town" if the Internet offers no roads leading us to this place. The dark web is more of an underground dungeon that you can only access through certain hidden passageways.

There are two facets to this hidden part of the Internet: the deep web and the dark web. Think of the places you go—Google, Amazon, Facebook—as residents of the "surface web" or "clear web." They all invite the public through simple dot-com addresses. Pornhub is part of the clear web. It's not hidden at all.

The deep web is only accessible through much more complicated IP (Internet protocol) addresses, perhaps also with password protection. Much of the content found in the deep web is legitimate: your email; cloud storage, that "place" where you store files safely rather than simply in your home or office; banking information and other daily transactional data that happens through the

24. Nicholas Kristof, "The Children of Pornhub," *The New York Times*, December 4, 2020, https://www.nytimes.com/2020/12/04/opinion/sunday/pornhub-rape-trafficking.html?action=click&module=RelatedLinks&pgtype=Article.

Internet, but privately. Most of us use the deep web every day. It's like the overhead compartment near your airplane seat that keeps the necessary stuff out of the way.

Hidden within that deep web is a darker passage, however. This is where many of the worst problems lie, including human trafficking, drug trafficking, and nearly any kind of crime imaginable. Once you know where to find the door, entry is simple. That entry is called Tor, which stands for The Onion Router. Tor is a browser, like Google Chrome, Firefox, or Microsoft Edge. It offers access to the overlay network with underground activity known as the dark web. Of key importance is that Tor provides anonymity.

If you download music or a movie illegally on the clear web, you can quickly be identified and held accountable. Your IP address is visible. However, through tools such as Tor, users can make transactions without being identified. It's like wearing a full disguise and going to the side of town where there are no security cameras, no police on duty, and no one interested in asking your identity. After taking its percentage, an ATM in this side of town exchanges standard money for Bitcoin, meaning people can then buy any kind of narcotics, sell human beings for slavery, or even a contract killer to eliminate an enemy.

Tor is the gateway to that side of town, where it's always the dead of night and never morning—and where a maze of marketplaces can be found. Yet *onion routing*, the architecture on which Tor is built, was crafted by United States Naval Research Laboratory scientists in the mid-nineties, just as the Internet was becoming all the rage in American culture. The purpose was benign: to create secure channels for American intelligence communications. Spy talk couldn't happen in email or amidst other online traffic.

The Tor network used encryption that worked in layers, like an onion. It takes one's internet address (IP) and relays the signal worldwide, thus obscuring its origin. For example, a person surfing the web in the United States might appear to be surfing the web in Estonia. While it protected US intelligence, it also threw off investigators seeking to locate the source of an illegal transaction.

The program was introduced to the public in 2003. It wasn't long before the network's secrecy potential was co-opted for its crime potential.

THE TWISTED PATH OF SILK ROAD

There are many sites on the dark web, but one site has become well known.

In 2011, an obscure user, Dread Pirate Roberts, turned up on the dark web and created and operated a market website called Silk Road. His choices of names were suggestive: Dread Pirate Roberts was a comical character in the film *The Princess Bride*. In the movie, almost anyone could accept the job as the Dread Pirate Roberts. The Silk Road refers to an international trade route between Europe and China used in the ancient world. So the originator's thinking was clear: he saw himself as a pirate using a pseudonym that might well be someone else at any given time and one who operated a wide-spanning market for goods of all types.

During its first two years, the site developed listings of ten thousand products for sale by anonymous vendors. Almost three quarters of the transactions involved narcotics. However, one could also buy a fake driver's license. Anything that "harmed" another person (as if drugs could not) was not to be listed on Silk Road, including child exploitation material, hired murder, firearms, and stolen credit cards. Dread Pirate Roberts professed to be a strict libertarian who believed in market freedom—up to a point. However, the many competitor sites that popped up, like Black Market Reloaded, had no such restrictions.

How could one trust anonymous sellers? They could read the reviews left by other buyers, just as an Amazon shopper might do. User forums also allowed helpful discussion, such as instructions on how to ship items to defy tracing.

For two years, Silk Road flew beneath the public radar. But then Gawker published an article about the site's goings-on, and the world began to pay attention. Soon US Senator Charles Schumer requested that the Drug Enforcement Agency and the Justice Department shut down the site. Someone attempted to do that, using a Denial of Service attack to knock Silk Road offline. Hackers use this strategy to flood a site with artificial traffic that weighs down the site and makes it unavailable. But in a short period, Silk Road was back, selling drugs and other items.

In June of 2013, the Drug Enforcement Agency seized 11.02 bitcoins—the equivalent at that moment of $814. What was more significant was that the bitcoins came from a Silk Road transaction. The buyer wasn't very cautious; he was tracked after the Bitcoin wallet was identified and followed, and the man was arrested for intent to sell drugs illegally. Once again, "follow the money" eventually paid off.

In October of that year, authorities took Dread Pirate Roberts into custody thanks to the work of Detective Gary Alford. Alford did some Googling. He searched for uses of the .onion URL address or .tor itself on the mainstream Internet, where the journey begins for everyone who ends up buying or selling on the dark web. From there, Alford followed the trail, looking for someone who may have originally promoted the site. The earliest mention of .onion came from a user named "altoid." Sure enough, searches for "altoid" usernames led him to solicitations for an open business opportunity. The personal email of Ross Ulbricht was given. As Ulbricht became a suspect, he seemed to be a reasonable match for the profile sought. Further investigation found him living under an alias in the San Francisco area.

It was important to tie Ulbricht, who took great precautions, to the Dread Pirate Roberts handle. Ulbricht performed Silk Road activities on his laptop and moved frequently, logging on only in public places with Wi-Fi. Eventually, a federal agent managed to infiltrate the Dread Pirate Robert's circle; he corresponded regularly with Dread Pirate Roberts online, determined to get Ulbricht to log on while he was under surveillance—which would powerfully prove the alias.

Ulbricht was ultimately located at a public library in San Francisco when his online identity popped up. Given how careful Ulbricht had been, agents feared that he would quickly delete or encrypt his files at the last second when he realized he was being seized. Therefore, a couple of agents pretended to engage in a loud lovers' quarrel at a nearby table to grab Ulbricht's attention. Then, other agents quickly arrested him and read him his rights. Another agent grabbed Ulbricht's laptop, inserted a flash drive, and quickly copied the essential files.

The suspect was indicted on a lengthy series of charges, most of which involved narcotics trafficking, though one charge involved murder-for-hire. He was convicted on all counts other than the murder conspiracy, which was dropped. Ulbricht was given a double life sentence plus forty years and was required to pay $183 million in restitution.

Who was this scourge of the Internet? An Eagle Scout with a master's degree in material science and engineering—a bright, well-liked thirty-year-old who looked like the proverbial guy next door. He just happened to facilitate one billion dollars worth of drug deals on his site and was charged with personally ordering six murders.

Open Internet activists helped to pay for his defense; they believed this was a matter of online freedom.

HOW FREE IS FREEDOM?

The ongoing debate is how much of the Internet can be monitored and controlled. The advocates of Open Internet, or Net Neutrality, insist that those online should have freedom without controls or censorship. Most Americans favorably respond to that general idea, particularly given our devotion to the First Amendment. Freedom is a key American principle—perhaps *the* key principle. However, nations like China heavily censor their Internet traffic, squelching important voices.

During the 1990s, a massive number of Americans learned their way around cyberspace. This new medium was seen as an expression of democracy, of people being able to post their interests and their opinions without a filter. However, questions inevitably arose as the worst elements of society began to abuse the freedom of information technology. Silk Road was just one prominent example.

A landmark attempt to create a safer Internet came before Congress during the period when the Backpage site was shut down. The longer name of the act was Allow States and Victims to Fight Online Sex Trafficking Act of 2017. It passed with a vote of 388 to 25, which signified a rare occasion when both political parties agreed on an item of legislation.

This was seen as a matter of practicality over idealism. Freedom of speech is a beautiful thing until it's abused in a way that brings terrible danger to our children. That's why there are necessary limits to our constitutionally protected right to speak freely. Certain types of speech aren't protected under the First Amendment, like defamation, true threats, fighting words, obscenity, child pornography, and commercial advertising.

Over the years, laws have been passed or tweaked to make reasonable exceptions for those issues when safety is threatened or the community is harmed. FOSTA revisited Section 230 of the Communications Decency Act, which protected online services from civil liability for the actions of their users. The earlier version of the Decency Act offered broad immunity to Internet companies that many of these companies made no effort to clean up the illegal activity they were enabling. Traffic was commerce, so they looked the other way. Under the Decency Act, if someone threatened your life over Comcast email, it was not Comcast's fault, and Comcast wouldn't be held accountable.

Under the new act, accountability was changing in certain cases. The new act underlined national sex trafficking laws, stating that it was illegal to knowingly assist, facilitate, or support sex trafficking. Therefore, someone like Ross Ulbricht could not open a website and claim that it wasn't his problem if millions of dollars of illegal narcotics were sold there.

The immediate effect of the legislation was that the dark web's purveyors of criminal commerce moved offshore, where American legislation couldn't touch them. A few sites and servers were busted in the United States, but even an act by Congress can't stop what goes on across the oceans in nations with lax Internet supervision.

PORNHUB TRAFFICKING

While taking down Silk Road was a great victory in the general fight to defeat the most influential purveyors of the dark web, it's important to remember that Dread Pirate Roberts's site didn't involve itself in human trafficking. It was mostly about narcotics and false IDs (though we know that, in this world, major crimes tend to be entangled with each other). What the investigative success of the Silk Road case may have done was to prove that, ultimately, anyone who leaves any digital footprint can eventually be located. And at Dark Watch, we endorse that idea.

You don't need to download a Tor browser and descend to the murky depths of the dark web to find trafficking and other crimes. Even with Backpage shut down, there are still mainstream websites where sex trafficking is being enabled. For instance, Pornhub is a Canadian site that draws more visitors than Amazon and many other popular website destinations. It trends among the most visited websites in the world.[25] As the name indicates, it's a massive archive of pornographic videos, much of which is uploaded by users.

Since videos earn money for viewings, as on YouTube, site profiteers attempt to upload the most lurid, sensational films and images. Therefore, alleged rape videos—including child exploitation—are a lucrative business for some people. It's possible to search by age range, so "girls under 18" is a popular category. Occasionally, outright child abuse is filmed and hosted on Pornhub. Given the profitability of pornography, Pornhub creates new incentives for the traffickers.

In late 2020, *New York Times* opinion columnist Nicholas Kristof attracted a great deal of public dialogue when he profiled some of the real people who had appeared on Pornhub. One of them was Serena Fleites, whose story opened this chapter. Another anecdote concerned a mother who finally located her missing daughter, age fifteen, on the Pornhub site—to the tune of fifty-eight separate sex videos. When charges were filed, the site managed to retain immunity for hosting the videos.

Pornhub often denies it accepts depictions of minors, but who can tell exactly how old an anonymous female in a film might be? It can be challenging to identify the personalities and determine illegality. In some cases, blurred faces in the videos intentionally hide the age of the participants.

Cali was one of the women who spoke to Kristof in the *Times* piece. She identified Pornhub as her trafficker. A family in the United States adopted her as a child from her home in China, only to place her into sex trafficking, particularly to produce videos. Her ordeal began when she was nine years old. She said that some of the videos continued to cycle through Pornhub years later.

---

25. "Top Websites Ranking," Similarweb, April 1, 2024, https://www.similarweb.com/top-websites/.

Cali managed to escape the nightmare of human slavery that her American experience had become and was attending college with high ambitions—but her history of sex videos always cast a shadow over her life. Just knowing her images were out there, still being leered at, gave her deep, ongoing anxiety.

Pornhub and similar porn sites have benefitted from videos showing abuse, rape, and other forms of sexually degrading violence. While they've publicly committed to identifying and removing illegal content from their site, their popularity and profit stream remains strong.

However, after Kristof's shocking story, there was talk of holding the credit card companies responsible for helping enable criminal activity. Three credit card companies disallowed their services to be used on Pornhub; that was a start.

In 2021, more than thirty women sued the pornographic website, accusing it of being a "classic criminal enterprise" monetizing rape, child exploitation materials, and sex trafficking. Untold numbers of women, they claimed, were being exploited daily. The suit went against MindGeek, the parent company of not only Pornhub but an extensive network of similar sites. One of the plaintiffs was Serena Fleites, who was becoming an icon of resistance against this crime.

The suit underlined the patterns of organized crime in the running of the sites, including the use of shell companies for laundering the incoming cash. The attorney for the plaintiffs said that Pornhub was abusing these women over and over, with each view, as long as those videos remain posted.[26] The suit was eventually settled for an undisclosed sum.

---

26. Marisa Iati, "Pornhub profits from rape, child pornography and sex trafficking, dozens of women allege in lawsuit," *The Washington Post*, June 18, 2021, https://www.washingtonpost.com/business/2021/06/18/pornhub-lawsuit-rape-child-porn-sex-trafficking/.

What if more victims begin to file these suits? Pressuring these sites and the companies that oversee them with legal and financial action is another weapon for the public to use in a growing arsenal against trafficking and abuse.

The Internet will continue to be a place where trafficking and other criminal activities take place. We can't prevent foreign sites from being accessible unless those nations cooperate by holding their local websites accountable. We can't stop people from being tempted toward what becomes a life-wrecking pornography addiction—one that is easier than ever to feed.

As parents and citizens, however, we can monitor our family's Internet use, whether on PCs, tablets, or phones. We can also talk with them about the dangers, sharing true and cautionary stories like the ones in this chapter. Our children need to know that supervision and protection are the duties of love and that we will make any sacrifice to keep them from the dangers that lurk in the netherworld of the dark net and the clear net.

12

JEFFREY EPSTEIN AND THE ELITE TRAFFICKERS

Say what you want about Jeffrey Epstein—and by now, plenty has been said—but he had an incredible power to get what he wanted out of people. His ability to attain sufficient power while exhibiting insufficient personal morality shows us that society has a problem. The scandal that led to his fall was felt among the worldwide social, financial, and political elite.

As a young man, Epstein taught at a prestigious school, even though he did not hold a college degree. He seemed like a nice, wholesome person from a quiet, gentle family.[27] He was considered a nerd and a math whiz. However, he also exhibited inappropriate behavior toward female students. Eventually he was dismissed for his performance, only to land a job at Bear Stearns (the powerful investment bank that helped to set off a financial cataclysm when it failed in 2008).

27. Michael Daly, "Epstein's Coney Island Days: From Math Nerd to 'Arrogant' Prick," *The Daily Beast*, August 19, 2019, https://www.thedailybeast.com/jeffrey-epsteins-coney-island-days-from-math-nerd-to-arrogant-prick.

Epstein found continued success by networking with some of the parents at the school that fired him. Networking—that's where he excelled, from all appearances. He moved up in a high-pressure environment where he was competing with the best and the brightest. He started with a menial assistant job in 1976 and quickly became an options trader, working with some of the firm's wealthiest clients. By 1980, he was a limited partner.

The following year, Epstein was fired for a trading violation, but his career continued to flourish. His next job was running his own financial business. He continued to work for wealthy clients and governments, seeking to recover money embezzled or cheated away. However, there are indications he worked in shady financial realms himself.

He networked in influential circles and socialized with presidents, kings, and oligarchs.[28] He said so himself on occasion. When his company Towers Financial was exposed for a massive Ponzi scheme in 1993, losing almost half a billion dollars of other people's money, somehow Epstein walked away without being charged with investor fraud. There are perks to being among the elite.

In 1996, he relocated his current firm to the US Virgin Islands, where it could enjoy every privilege of the American banking network while reducing his taxes by ninety percent.[29]

During the financial crisis, he suffered monetary losses, just as other billionaires and corporations did. By this time, he had other problems as well. He was under federal investigation for abuse of underage girls. Epstein had moved beyond the groups and contacts that dealt with business success; he had become a trafficker of young girls.

---

28. John Schindler, "It Sure Looks Like Jeffrey Epstein Was a Spy—But Whose?" *Observer*, July 10, 2019, https://observer.com/2019/07/jeffrey-epstein-spy-intelligence-work/.
29. Tom Metcalf, Greg Farrell, and David Kocieniewski, "The Jeffrey Epstein Guide to Cutting Your Tax Bill by 90%," *Bloomberg*, July 28, 2019, https://www.bloomberg.com/news/articles/2019-07-27/the-jeffrey-epstein-guide-to-cutting-your-tax-bill-by-90.

HEAVY TRAFFIC

As far as anyone has discovered, Epstein was sexually abusing minors as early as 2000. It happened at his New York and Palm Beach homes and on his island paradise in the US Virgin Islands. In time, the process grew more systematic, but in the beginning, he would ask the girl to visit; then, he would request a back massage. The massages were Epstein's gateway to illegal sexual activity. Epstein would pay his victims generously, letting them know it wouldn't be good for anyone if the encounter between them were discussed. If the girl seemed okay with things, he might ask her if she had any friends who would like to make some money too. Epstein saved the girls' names and numbers—at least if they were still young enough to please him. In time, he accumulated such a long contact list of young girls that, wherever his more typical business might carry him, he could make a phone call or two and have a girl waiting to fulfill his every desire.

We read about this pattern and wonder how it could have gone undetected and unprosecuted as long as it did. Depending upon the secrecy of teenage girls—some of whom were not "okay with things"—seems like a reckless way to go for a wealthy man. Unfortunately, money and power can create an air of invincibility for the elite; anything is possible when you're friends with people in high places.

In 2005, authorities in Florida began investigating the claims of a fourteen-year-old girl who said she'd been sexually exploited at Epstein's Palm Beach mansion. The investigation pulled at a thread that started to unravel the whole sordid tapestry. Several other girls came forward, all of whom told the same story about sexual massages and lucrative payoffs. Eventually, authorities charged Epstein with a single count of soliciting prostitution—a drastic understatement of the human trafficking the billionaire had been up to for at least several years.

Amidst public criticism of judicial leniency, the US attorney in Miami negotiated for months with the Epstein team of high-powered lawyers. His attorneys contended that the girls were lying, and a plea bargain was offered. In June of 2008, Epstein offered guilty pleas to two minimal charges, one for soliciting prostitution and the other for soliciting "underaged prostitution."[30] He received an eighteen-month jail sentence, during which he was allowed to work at his office during the day and return to jail at night. The secret deal allowed him to miss out entirely on federal charges.

The Federal Bureau of Investigation got involved and confirmed reports of forty minors. A reporter for the *Miami Herald* dug deeper, finding eighty victims, sixty of whom she was able to locate.[31] The *Miami Herald* reporting created a national story. As readers learned about the case, the inadequacy of the punishment created a public outcry, at least in some quarters, about what was a slap on the wrist for a serial pedophilic rapist. Women continued to come forward, and the stories they told opened up frightening possibilities that went far beyond one billionaire money manager and his sick proclivities. Virginia Giuffre, for example, filed a suit claiming that, at the age of seventeen, she was trafficked by Epstein for sexual appointments with wealthy, powerful, and sometimes famous men. One of them was alleged to be Prince Andrew, a member of the British royal family. Politicians, tycoons, attorneys, and other social and cultural elite members were also named. One name was repeatedly tied to these stories: Ghislaine Maxwell.

THE PROCURER

I once spoke to an Epstein survivor. She was rebuilding her life after the devastation of abuse at the hands of a sexual predator

---

30. *Underaged prostitution* is an outdated term. The law calls any commercial sex with a minor by its proper crime, *human trafficking*.
31. Julie Brown, "For Years, Jeffrey Epstein Abused Teen Girls, Police Say. A Timeline of His Case," *Miami Herald*, November 28, 2018, https://www.miamiherald.com/news/local/article221404845.html..

in that time of life that is already so difficult for children—the borderland between childhood and adulthood. The young lady described the grooming process, mainly carried out by Ghislaine Maxwell, who knew exactly how to procure and prepare young girls to be used and discarded.

Maxwell was a mysterious and central player in Jeffrey Epstein's sad saga. She was a former romantic interest of Epstein who continued to run the household personnel decisions. She had the flexibility to manage Epstein's home and business affairs, to serve as a ready date with plenty of sophistication at cocktail parties, and to recruit and groom teenage girls without ever showing any guilt. She even piloted the helicopter that carried Epstein to his private island.

Maxwell's charisma was probably the most crucial reason Epstein worked with her so long. It was the key to her success. Girls saw this socialite with a British accent as everything they aspired to be. She was wealthy and articulate, flying worldwide on a private jet, and seemed to care about girls. She gained the girls' trust and clearly and carefully explained what Epstein desired.

Virginia Giuffre was working as a spa attendant when she first met Maxwell. Maxwell approached her and commented on the massage therapy book the girl was reading. After they conversed, Maxwell offered her a job as a traveling masseuse for Jeffrey Epstein. Giuffre made the mistake of telling the couple she had been sexually abused in the past. After this disclosure, Maxwell and Epstein targeted and preyed upon her vulnerability.

At Epstein's home, the billionaire waited in a reclined position, nude. Maxwell trained Giuffre in how to properly massage the money manager. After that, he and Maxwell began grooming Giuffre to be trafficked among his friends. She would travel as a supposed massage specialist, but her true job description was all about sex. For nearly three years, she traveled on private jets being "passed around like a platter of fruit," as she put it, among Epstein's circle of friends.[32]

There were plenty of other girls, of course. Those who came forward inevitably described how Ghislaine Maxwell groomed them and trained them to give Epstein exactly what he wanted. If there were problems, Maxwell cleaned things up. She scouted for new girls, but the most reliable method of adding to the network was having the girls bring in recruits. As they visited for the first time, usually nervous and hesitant, Epstein appeared to be a kind uncle, a mentor for young people. He sat with them and discussed life in general, asked about their goals, and then inquired whether they'd be so kind as to rub his back. But on return visits, the relationship began to change. He might continue to pay the usual three hundred dollars, but he made demands, and the sex was abusive.

Virginia Giuffre's lawsuit in 2015 finally began to bring the issue to a head. In 2016, more young women came forward. Generally they settled for undisclosed amounts of cash, but by this time, there was a more serious federal investigation taking place. In July of 2019, Epstein was finally arrested on federal sex trafficking charges. He was placed in a federal jail in New York City, where it was ruled he died by suicide.

One year later, Ghislaine Maxwell was also charged with sex crimes, particularly for the recruitment of young girls for sexual purposes. For months, she was a fugitive and could not be located. But, once again, technology came to the rescue. She was located and arrested in Bradford, New Hampshire, in July of 2020 through the use of a *stingray*, an IMSI-catcher mobile phone tracking device. Maxwell was on a call with her attorneys when she was located.

---

32. "Virginia Giuffre: What we know about Prince Andrew's accuser," *BBC*, January 12, 2022, https://www.bbc.co.uk/news/world-us-canada-59974220.

Maxwell was found guilty on five sex trafficking related counts by a jury four days after Christmas in 2021. She received twenty years for her sentence.

Ultimately, she had neither family nor Epstein money, and she had to sue the Epstein estate for backpay to pay her attorneys. In time, they sued her for lack of payment. Maxwell was no longer "elite," no longer wealthy, no longer facing anything but the walls and iron bars of confinement during her declining years.

Jeffrey Epstein's horrific story should confirm once and for all that, yes, there is human trafficking among the wealthy and powerful—the elite. When Epstein's story is examined, his is not the only powerful name that arises. American politicians, a member of the British royal family, sports figures, and business icons were also mentioned.

MYTH AND REALITY

When the incredible becomes credible, we become open to believing almost anything. That is a problem. What if a genuine crisis is used to introduce mythological elements? What if stories are passed around through social media that mix truth and fiction, so we ultimately don't know what to believe?

In recent years, a self-professed investigator walked into a pizza parlor in Washington, DC. He had been "briefed" on the Internet about a child sex ring that operated out of the restaurant. After spending three days reading articles on Pizzagate and watching convincing YouTube videos devoted to the subject, he had attempted to gather a kind of posse to go exact justice, but nobody else would go with him. So, with his AR-15 in hand, he drove from his home in North Carolina, angry and passionate, to singlehandedly free the captive children being held by a Satan-worshipping, child-abusing cult connected to a political party.

As he entered the parlor, he immediately saw a good number of children—many of whom saw the huge rifle and the loaded revolver at his hip and began to run out the door with their parents. The man started examining the walls and tables, looking for the basement door that led to the Satanic activities. He shot through a door, ruining a computer.

The man was apologetic in his plea bargain request. He had fallen prey to a well-packaged, massively accepted Internet hoax.[33]

The national recounting of the story brought forth much talk about social media fiction and the credibility of people. These were significant topics. But what happens when a "boy who cried wolf" scenario occurs? Once the Internet's many false accusations about elite sex factories are disregarded, will people recognize a true crisis when it crosses their path? How about the local illicit massage parlor just around the corner, where women are trafficked every day? Probably no elites are involved. The story lacks the drama of Satan-worshippers in the basement of a pizza parlor abusing children. But it's *real*.

Ironically, the arrest and death of Epstein, while spreading the word about the awful realities of trafficking, helped encourage several urban legends and false stories. The movie *Taken*, which inspired millions of others and me, left us with a tendency to Hollywoodize our thinking on this issue. In an age of polarized politics, people inevitably seized on such a powerful and emotional issue to connect their political agendas to false stories that inevitably link the political opponent to human trafficking.

Internet discussion will never bear the solid credibility of a set of bound encyclopedias. It's a network of ordinary human voices who often see what they want to see or believe what they should be questioning. All we can do is be vigilant in separating truth from

---

33. Merrit Kennedy, "'Pizzagate' Gunman Sentenced To 4 Years In Prison," *NPR*, June 22, 2017, https://www.npr.org/sections/thetwo-way/2017/06/22/533941689/pizzagate-gunman-sentenced-to-4-years-in-prison.

fiction. We read in 1 John 4:1, *"Beloved, believe not every spirit, but try the spirits whether they are of God: because many false prophets are gone out into the world"* (KJV). The word *try* is probably more accurately rendered as *test*. John is pointing out that there are many spirits in the world, and there are plenty of false prophets spreading the wrong ones.

The Spirit of God gives us the ability to discern the godly from the ungodly, but we must be alert. We feel deep emotion about what is happening to people worldwide in this trafficking phenomenon. We feel anger at the transgressors and compassion toward the victims. However, we have to be certain that Christ is at the center of our interactions—and that He is never part of propaganda and falsehood. So even as we see the terrible truth in stories like the Epstein saga, we must test the spirits when other stories come to us.

We also need to remember that God is in control. For many years, it seemed as if Epstein and his circle escaped justice even after an FBI investigation, even after abusing scores of girls. We're tempted to say there's one kind of justice for ordinary people and another for the elite and the powerful. Numbers 32:23 offers us another powerful promise to claim: *"Be sure your sin will find you out"* (KJV). This is a clear pattern throughout the Scriptures: evil people seem to escape punishment, and justice seems to have fallen asleep—but God never sleeps. (See Psalm 121:4.) In time, His judgment arrives, both in this world and the next. This verse doesn't mean we should turn away and be passive as we let God handle things; we are His instruments, His tools for working in this world and bringing in His kingdom. The point is that we can't afford to grow bitter and cynical. He will bring full and final justice according to His timetable. We must ask, "What can I do to help on this day?"

13

THE SLOW-MOTION SEDUCTION
OF SEXUAL GROOMING

The 2022 TV series *A Friend of the Family* dramatized an actual and inexplicable event. In 1972, Robert Berchtold and his wife befriended the Broberg family, who had just moved into their neighborhood. After meeting at a church service, the two families became nearly inseparable. Robert was fantastic with the Broberg kids, full of fun and laughter, and took a keen interest in them: volunteering to drive them to school regularly and taking them on camping trips. In fact, he seemed to spend more time with them than he did with his own family.

As time passed, Robert developed a particularly close friendship with young Jan Broberg, age twelve. He offered her expensive gifts and was physically affectionate. He became someone Jan could confide in and get a warm hug from when needed. The inappropriate nature of the relationship was clear. In fact, Robert confessed his obsession with Jan to church officials. Then, amazingly, he managed to convince everyone—including Jan's parents—that the therapeutic key to facing his obsession with Jan and overcoming it was to sleep in her bedroom with her—just the two of them and no one else.

Later, the Brobergs explained that "B," as they called Berchtold, had earned their trust. It just couldn't be a sexual thing—not someone like B! It never crossed their minds that he was anything but a second father who had a special connection with one of their kids. In their all-American, churchgoing existence, there were some things, sick things, that good people like them didn't need to worry about.

When the relationship was in real danger of being detected by the naïve Brobergs, B maneuvered himself into sexual affairs with both of Jan's parents—a variation on sextortion. The guilt-ridden husband and wife were silenced by the threat that B would reveal the affairs if they began to ask questions about what was going on between him and their daughter. Now the whole family was under B's control.

Eventually, Robert kidnapped Jan not once, but twice—once when she was twelve, and the next time when she was fourteen— and married her. It took years for her parents to get her home again, and when they did, it was as if a cult had brainwashed her. She wanted to be with her abuser. Only love, patience, and endurance helped Jan understand and heal from Robert's emotional, mental, physical, and sexual abuse.[34]

Jan went on to become a successful actress in TV and movies and a spokesperson for the problems of sexual abuse and pedophilia in America. She also stands as a case study of how sly and powerful the grooming process can be.

---

34. Austin Harvey, "The Disturbing Story of Robert Berchtold, The Pedophile Who Kidnapped And Assaulted His Neighbors' Daughter—Twice," All That's Interesting, September 26, 2022, https://allthatsinteresting.com/robert-berchtold.

GENTLE PERSUASION

Grooming, for generations, was the most innocuous of words. The word means something else entirely now. It has come to carry the connotation of exploiting a minor through a trusting relationship for nonconsensual sexual activity.[35]

When researchers began seriously studying the psychology of sexual abuse about sixty years ago, they made a careful distinction between types of abuse. There was a difference between pressured sex and forced sex.[36] The commonly held idea of the rapist had been someone lurking in a dark alley, pouncing on a female victim, physically overpowering her, and committing rape. That was forced sex, often viewed as a crime of violence rather than desire. Anger, not lust, is the prime motivator. But pressured sex is different. It's less a crime of anger than one of cunning and manipulation. The rapist is playing the long game. Predators of this type find the carrot to be more effective than the stick—this is because enticement, rewards, and flattery will work more often than brute force.

During the eighties, researcher Ken Lanning began to use the term that has taken hold: *grooming*.[37] In the last few decades, we've discovered, to our horror, that the sexual predator is less likely to be a guy in the alley, and *more* likely to be a family member, a worker in a nursery or church, or a trusted friend. That's not an encouraging thought. The enemy is not "out there somewhere," but possibly close to our family circle.

Grooming is subtle and can pass for simple care and nurturing. The predator is building trust with children, but for perverted

35. Merriam-Webster.com Dictionary, s.v. "groom," accessed April 19, 2024, https://www.merriam-webster.com/dictionary/groom.
36. "Out of Mind, Out of Sight: Breaking down the barriers to understanding child sexual exploitation," Child Exploitation and Online Protection Centre, June 2011, https://web.archive.org/web/20140523010403/http://www.ceop.police.uk/Documents/ceopdocs/ceop_thematic_assessment_executive_summary.pdf.
37. Ken Lanning, "The Evolution of Grooming: Concept and Term," *Journal of Interpersonal Violence*, 33 (1), 5–16, https://doi.org/10.1177/0886260517742046.

purposes. Today, any institution that cares for children is far more likely than in the past to run a background check for any hire. It's a legal requirement for childcare providers. This is true not only because abuse has become more prevalent but also because we're more aware it was a hidden, undiscussed problem all along. How much sexual abuse occurred in the past, only to remain suppressed and hidden from public view?

In the eighties, we began to wake up. But as often happens, a certain amount of hysteria surrounded the dawning realization that abusers were a more significant problem than once understood. Nurseries and daycare centers everywhere came under heavy suspicion, often through false accusations that mushroomed into public panic. The McMartin trials are the most famous example.[38] There was an uproar when a child seemed to describe a sexual encounter and when other children were asked about their own experiences with leading questions. There's an art to getting accurate answers from children, who often try to say what they sense adults want to hear.

In the McMartin case, massive misunderstandings abounded. Rational thinking returned, but it was a new day. Healthy hiring processes were put into practice. Registration of sex offenders became federally mandated in 1994.[39]

But the environment of predatory behavior changed during the same period. The Internet was then becoming a factor, and there was no vetting in the cyber world. Anyone with a computer now had a vast stalking ground. Chat rooms became a dangerous

38. David Shaw, "Where Was Skepticism in Media? Pack journalism and hysteria marked early coverage of the McMartin case. Few Journalists stopped to question the believability of the prosecution's charges," *The Los Angeles Times*, January 19, 1990, https://www.latimes.com/archives/la-xpm-1990-01-19-mn-226-story.html.
39. "Legislative History of Federal Sex Offender Registration and Notification," Office of Sex Offender Sentencing, Monitoring, Apprehending, Registering, and Tracking, US Department of Justice, accessed August 10, 2023, https://smart.ojp.gov/sorna/current-law/legislative-history.

habitat for grooming. The predator could create an identity and build confidence in a relationship.

PREDATORY PRACTICES

Grooming has now become a popular term used primarily in a negative sense. There is grooming for sexual abuse or for joining a terrorist group. You could be groomed for a political office or business leadership. But mostly it means slow, exploitation for nonconsensual sexual purposes.

By this time, the grooming process has become a subject of study, and we can be aware of the patterns it follows, though every situation is a bit different. We've already come across the phrase *pig-butchering*, but the catch-all idea for all these concepts is grooming because stealth is at the core. Even older children are unlikely to fall off a steep cliff, but a slippery slope is something else—an easy descent that just as surely leads to the bottom.

Let's examine some of the common patterns of groomers.

1. **The predator finds a victim.** Nearly any child might be a target, though it helps if the predator has ready access to the victim. In our chapter-opening illustration, Robert Berchtold was a friend of the family—a close one. He had natural access to the child he targeted, and he was able to create plenty of opportunities for abuse. For teenagers and older victims, pictures on social media may be the trigger. Predators may be attracted to certain types of victims. The critical point is that predators find targets and focus all their resources on attaining access to those targets.

2. **The predator gains access.** The predator crosses paths with the victim by some method, attempting to be as harmless as possible. We're way past the stereotype of the man in the unmarked van offering candy. Predators

will find ways to gain logical access to the playground, the school hallway, or even the family. They'll play a part of some kind. The Internet is an easy way for predators to access teens and older victims.

3. **The predator gains trust.** Gaining trust is a skill, but not a difficult one. We meet and then get to know strangers all the time. On social media, it's possible to pose and strike up a friendship. Warmth and listening skills create an atmosphere of trust. The predator may seem extremely trustworthy at some point—but they aren't. Gaining trust is essential because, once we trust someone, we're willing to ride with them in a car or be alone in a room with them.

The most effective grooming technique is to get involved in the child's life, as Berchtold did. In time, he was indistinguishable from a beloved uncle. Jan and the other children came to him for guidance and advice.

Parents or friends—those who see themselves as watching out for us—gain the highest level of trust. A sexual predator can be extremely patient, working for months to gain just enough credibility for that opportunity to strike. Parents and friends often doubt the inevitable accusations: "I just won't believe a nice person like _____ did something like that. This had to be a misunderstanding of some kind."

4. **The predator gives lots of gifts.** Everyone likes being surprised by a wonderful present of some kind. Children respond powerfully to candy, toys, a new phone, or a computer game. For someone older, it could be money, drugs, or a modeling opportunity. "Talent scouts" spot teenage girls at the mall with "that special look" and offer to snap a few quick photos—perhaps outside, near

that pretty tree next to the parking lot (and the preda-tor's vehicle).

5. **The predator lures the victim from safe bounds.** There must come a point at which the predator and the victim are in a position for the predator to take the desired action. Everything up to this point has been a chess game played by only one side. We protect our children much more actively today than parents did in previous generations, but a determined predator will find a gap somewhere, a sufficient opportunity to get the victim alone. This is much easier with older victims. Young women can be picked up from bars or public places. Again, the Internet provides the opportunity to create the right conditions. The occasion may come when the predator offers a gift or opportunity the victim needs to see in person. It could be the promise of backstage access for a popular concert.

    During the trust-building process, a sexual backdrop may be gradually introduced. For example, the predator may begin showing pornographic pictures to the victim, seemingly as a topic of conversation. He might ask, "I found this picture. What do you think about things like this?" It establishes the subject between them, and it can slowly build until it seems normal and less shocking.

    The predator may offer hugs and kisses on the cheek, slowly creating a physical closeness. Introducing tickling as a form of play in the relationship is common, perhaps backrubs. Showering together and sleeping in the same bed, should a predator receive the opportunity, are also classic parts of the pattern.

6. **The predator calls for secrecy.** "Probably best not to tell your parents about this" are words we must train our children to hear as warning sounds. The predator will

always have a reason that's credible on the surface. "You know by now you can trust me, but your mom and dad don't know that. Would you like them to take away our friendship?"

Perhaps it's more like, "I'm looking forward to our photo session. But let's not allow the word to get out to any of your friends. They'll want to get in on it, they'll flood us with calls, and you have something special to lose—they don't. Keep our project between us, at least until we're booking you on photo shoots that will bring in serious cash!"

7. **The predator introduces sexual activity.** This moment can take any number of forms. Naïve children may not understand they've been abused, though the predator will instruct or threaten them not to mention what happened. A trafficker, on the other hand, is building a business and may already have drugged the victim and imprisoned her. The abuser posing as a fashion photographer might claim that he couldn't control himself, but that now it's a special relationship—one that must remain secret, of course—and he'll suggest repeat performances in the future. What happens from here depends upon the situation, but it's a dangerous moment.

8. **The predator establishes complete control.** Given the risks, the predator seeks to control the victim as closely as possible. Threats of violent response are one way to do this. Suggesting shame (as if this situation is the victim's fault) and the need for coverup is another. Predators may take extreme action by imprisoning or drugging their victim. Introducing a drug dependency requires time, but this is one of the most powerful methods of keeping a victim in line—"Walk away, and where will you get your next hit?" Moving victims around, from city to city

or between multiple local locations, is another way to keep the victim confused and afraid to resist.

HELPING OUR CHILDREN

The victim may become compliant with sexual behavior if the predator carefully and patiently performs the stages of grooming. The victim will suffer from a load of guilt and shame during and after their ordeal. They may not realize that the predator sought to psychologically manipulate them using grooming techniques. The power of manipulation can be difficult to withstand.

To make things worse, if the predator ends up in court, they may claim nothing was forced, and everything was consensual. Early in the book we discussed how difficult an environment the justice system is for abuse victims. They must relive their worst moments, perhaps while they are still confused by their actions and emotions. Parents and other adults must work to help these young people understand that they're victims and nothing more. It's not their fault.

We can help our children by being vigilant and carefully vetting every adult who enters their world, whether at school, church, teams, clubs, or in the neighborhood. We also need to have accurate discernment in recognizing the warning signs of groomers.

What adult seems to desire to be in your child's world? Do they comment on or focus on the child's physical appearance?

Do they try to open communication channels, such as emails or online venues, without checking with you as a parent?

Do they share secrets with your child and express an interest in driving the child somewhere, or isolating the child somehow?

What's happening online for your child? Are you aware of phone, tablet, and computer activity and interactions? Have you talked with your child about being extremely careful with Internet strangers, who may not be who they appear to be? Explain that "just wanting to play a computer game with me" may seem innocent enough, but it could be part of establishing trust that will later be abused.

Be conscious of the risks posed toward different age groups: nearly 99 percent of cases of online grooming target those ages thirteen to seventeen; the most dangerous age is thirteen to fourteen. Girls are the most likely targets, and cell phones are the most common contact point. Curious and adventurous children are at highest risk.[40]

Social media platforms such as Facebook are being monitored and challenged in court and by the Justice Department, and many of them are setting new standards to discourage online grooming. However, some sites, like TikTok, can't be monitored because they are based out of foreign countries. Parents should take extreme care in the decision to allow new sites and apps. TikTok uses an algorithm that determines what will most likely command its users' attention, and then it plays to the result, developing a nearly irresistible hold on children. Many observers see it as the current reigning threat for sexual abuse of children.

Instances of TikTok leading to threats of sexual abuse have already occurred. For example, a middle-aged Alabama man began exchanging messages with a fourteen-year-old girl from Texas. Others were able to see the romantic notes and called out warnings of inappropriate behavior. However, this didn't stop the man from taking a bus to Texas and meeting the girl in person. Soon he was arrested for sexual assault.[41]

---

40. Emily R. Munro, *The Protection of Children Online: A Brief Scoping Review to Identify Vulnerable Groups*, Childhood Wellbeing Research Centre, 2011.
41. "TikTok Looms as Growing Child-Exploitation Threat," National Criminal Justice Association, February 16, 2023, https://www.ncja.org/crimeandjusticenews/tiktok-looms-as-growing-child-exploitation-threat

Watch for these signs in your child:

- The child begins mentioning an adult who wants to spend time with them.
- The adult has some interesting pastime or hobby that is attractive to the child.
- The child has skipped school, clubs, or team practices.
- The child has shown less interest in and attention to same-age friends.
- The child wants to spend more time in his or her room, and/or online.
- The child shows up with gifts or possessions that can't be explained.
- The child suddenly seems evasive and tells more lies than in the past.
- The child is less affectionate with parents and doesn't want to spend time with them.

The idea of predators seeking to abuse our children is perhaps the most horrifying conception we can imagine. There's a natural resistance to wrapping our minds around it. But the worst possible response is to deny the possibility ("It can't happen to us!") and look the other way. We must be educated, vigilant, and attentive to how our children spend their time, online and after school. It's not always easy. What if your child is at home during the summer while you work? It takes a little more care and creativity, perhaps the help of relatives or neighbors. But every safeguard is worth the effort.

If you, the parent, take the proper precautions, your children will never be in the range of a predator. Maintain a relationship that establishes proper boundaries and plenty of love. Be sure your children know they can talk to you about anything on their minds—and they'll believe it if you show appropriate interest and attention when they come to you. Eating dinners together as a family is a great place to talk and keep up with each other.

The years we have with our children are very short. They fly by more quickly than we ever expect. It's reasonable for us to make our children and their safety our highest priority during those short and precious years.

14

TECHNOLOGY TO DEFEAT TRAFFICKING

In 2012, a young lady leaped from a New York City bedroom window and fell six floors to the pavement. Somehow, she survived. Why did she do it? For two excruciating days, a group of men had imprisoned her in that room and sexually assaulted her. Eventually, she saw a death-leap as preferable.

The New York City District Attorney's Office managed to capture the man who had imprisoned her and used her to make money for himself. His name was Benjamin Gaston. He was tried for human trafficking and other charges and sentenced to fifty years to life in prison.

How did they catch him? The district attorney gave a great deal of credit to an Internet search tool called Memex, developed by the Defense Advanced Research Project Agency (DARPA). The US Department of Defense had commissioned the software especially for tracking human traffickers, and it was one of the first technology-facing strategies assigned to that purpose. Memex scoured the dark web, searching for signs of trafficking. The software flagged any advertisement with the possibility of luring people into captivity and promoting sexual exploitation. The arrest was made using information from the woman's memory and Memex.

We've come a long way since then.

If you think about computer life in general and how far technology has progressed in the last decade or so—how much more sophisticated it is—then you'll have some idea of how much more complex and effective our current technology is. Computers are more powerful, and there are more and sharper minds figuring out strategies for using them.

It's essential that we keep improving our work, because technology is more central to trafficking than to almost any other crime.

Consider this: If you wanted to buy some cocaine, you wouldn't have much trouble figuring out how, even if you'd never done such a thing. Plenty of people are out there with the product and the desire to sell it. They tend to be found in certain neighborhoods of any given town. You probably have an idea of where you'd go. There is usually no big secret about where the buying and the selling takes place. As a matter of fact, it's important to dealers that everyone knows where to find them.

Human trafficking is different. The business model isn't the same at all. Since their business involves taking people into captivity, traffickers have to recruit human cargo using special means, usually through advertising or public solicitation of some kind. The buyers for human captives also have to be located, so that involves a certain amount of advertising as well. Somewhere on the Internet that information must be available—not too glaring, but not too hidden, either. This is business, and it's carried out most prominently on the Internet. At some point, traffickers have to venture onto some kind of web environment and make their intentions known.

When traffickers use the Internet to conduct business, Dark Watch has the opportunity to catch them.

The right technology is like a thousand good researchers—or more—all combing the Internet at great speed, dividing their labors perfectly, and quickly learning patterns the rest of us could never pick up. The meteoric rise of AI (artificial intelligence) comes with both positives and negatives. One of the positives is that it can spot hidden patterns on how and where human traffickers go about their work. Your newer programs might tell you, "This girl is being trafficked in the same hotel room as one we observed three weeks ago. We've IDed the room's details." It might say, "This group has moved its human cargo out of this particular massage parlor, but we know exactly where they've gone, because we assembled seventeen informational clues."

DARK WATCH

At Dark Watch, we believed that tech was the best weapon from the beginning. Now we're really seeing it come into its own; let's be thankful for that. Every statistical reading suggests that human trafficking is on the increase. The global pandemic failed to slow it down, though the Internet showed a great spike in recruitment during the period that strip clubs, foster homes, and schools—places targeted by traffickers—were less accessible. This demonstrates that human trafficking morphs and adapts along with society. Natural influences aren't going to stop it; we must do that by intention and counteraction.[42]

We've described how it's trending and how we're responding to the best of our knowledge. My conclusion is that if these criminals are setting out to recruit our children, then parents, school personnel, church members, and other good citizens must be recruited to

---

42. "Analysis of 2020 National Human Trafficking Hotline Data," Polaris Project, accessed August 15, 2023, https://polarisproject.org/2020-us-national-human-trafficking-hotline-statistics/.

fight back. We all have something we can do; it might be as simple as praying regularly, or as tangible as offering financial support to effective organizations. It might require persistence as we converse regularly with elected officials about devoting time and money to fight a problem that is destroying our communities. Some might even want to step forward and devote their careers and their talents to eliminating trafficking in our world.

Those of us at Dark Watch took a long look at what traffickers were doing and what was lacking in the efforts to stop them. First, we chose to be aggressive and proactive in going after the criminals the way we'd approach the drug industry: go after the supplier rather than the dealer. Find the supply channels and crush them.

Secondly, we chose to work through technology, which we felt offered the richest resources for identifying those criminals and bringing them to justice. The traffickers themselves would tell you, if forced to be truthful, that technology is their best tool. It stands to reason that technology holds the key to their defeat as well. It's encouraging to realize that new tools are appearing all the time. We must stay ahead of the traffickers in implementing them.

Dark Watch aims to address the problem of siloing through its data analytic services. We find a good many companies and agents in our industry all doing their own thing in their own "silos." Duplication of effort subtracts from our efficiency. My friend Samuel and I realized that we need to fight with a massive, well-integrated army rather than a profusion of independent militias. That way we can share our wisdom and our newest advances, and everyone can specialize in what they do best.

We work with law enforcement, offering tools designed for that area. We make training, data, and analytic services available so any given community can find its pockets of challenge and know how to respond.

Dark Watch preserves data from every geographic sector and identifies new trafficking hubs. Our partners subscribe to the service and consult the data for assistance.

In establishing Dark Watch, we adopted a for-profit model because it allowed us to contract with the US Defense Department. We were also able to partner with the many nonprofits out there without competing against grants. Samuel and I made a few sacrifices to get our organization up and running. Friends would invite us on weekend adventures, and we would have to decline. We realized we couldn't accomplish significant goals without paying a significant price. So we kept our noses to the grindstone and pushed forward.

ZEROING IN ON THE TARGET

Trying to launch our idea from vision to reality was often discouraging in the early period, and it was natural to have doubts. Maybe our vision was too simplistic, too broad. Perhaps other organizations had this problem covered, and we weren't needed.

In 2017 came our real first break. We closed our first project with a specialized military group to adopt our findings in human trafficking. It was never a given that we could convince government entities to pursue trafficking as a priority because these entities were focused on drugs and terrorism, and trafficking was seen simply as a component of those crimes. As we've seen, organized crime is a massive rolling stone that gathers strands of every other crime as it rushes along. Drugs are a part of trafficking. Terrorism makes use of it, too. Our task was to demonstrate that this one crime had a deep story of its own and was deserving of the attention of all who fight crime.

At the time, the terrorist organization Boko Haram was front and center in world news. This Islamist jihadist faction, based in Nigeria, was incredibly violent, killing tens of thousands of people.

In 2014, its soldiers kidnapped 276 schoolgirls from a secondary school in Chibok, Nigeria. A few of these girls managed to leap from the backs of trucks and escape via the highway. Eighty were exchanged for Boko Haram leaders who had been captured. We know that many of these were forced to convert to Islam and marry their captors.[43] Eight-two are still missing to this day.[44]

This kidnapping served as an example of the crossover between terrorism and trafficking. Drug trafficking and human trafficking were both central to Boko Haram's work.[45] Criminal enterprises are funded by other criminal enterprises; it has always been this way. But while cocaine, weaponry, or stolen goods can be lucrative in the market, human beings—boys, girls, refugees, orphans—are always in ready supply and have a higher exchange rate. Unfortunately, humans are the perfect merchandise: they are globally available and hold a high financial value. Our message to government agencies was, "If you want to fully understand terrorist organizations, you have to follow the money. And the money comes from trafficking: human, organ, and labor."

Our message began to come through. In 2017, our contract with the US government gave us the traction and public standing to gather one million dollars in investment. Now we were able to pursue our vision in earnest.

Dark Watch's first product release was called TRAK. It was a specialized tool built to scan the Internet and retrieve phone numbers and email addresses of likely criminal organizations—a form

---

43. Nina Strochlic, "Six years ago, Boko Haram kidnapped 276 schoolgirls. Where are they now?" *National Geographic*, February 11, 2020, https://www.nationalgeographic.com/magazine/article/six-years-ago-boko-haram-kidnapped-276-schoolgirls-where-are-they-now.
44. Stephanie Busari, "They were kidnapped from a boarding school 10 years ago. Hear their stories," *CNN*, April 14, 2024, https://www.cnn.com/2024/04/13/africa/chibok-girls-ten-years-as-equals-intl-cmd/index.html.
45. "Open briefing of the Counter-Terrorism Committee on 'The nexus between international terrorism and transnational organize crime,'" United Nations, October 8, 2018, https://www.un.org/securitycouncil/ctc/sites/www.un.org.securitycouncil.ctc/files/chairs-summary.pdf.

of open-source intelligence that was out there all along; someone only needed to create the capability of gathering it efficiently. A proprietary scraper, powered by artificial intelligence, aggregated, cleansed, and disseminated both internal and external data. Note that scammers and other criminals "scrape" the Internet all the time; X (formerly Twitter) made changes to discourage the harvesting of personal information. We were turning the technology against the abusers.

After TRAK, we built a tool called Dark Maps, which highlighted potential human trafficking hot spots within the United States. I described our popular map app earlier in the book. Since it readily reveals the problem areas in any neighborhood, you can imagine its popularity. Soon after our formal launch of Dark Watch, we were in dialogue with the FBI, Department of Homeland Security, Interpol, and even the United Nations.

NEW DIRECTIONS, FRESH DANGERS

In 2018, we received our first contract to support personal injury attorneys in pursuing lawsuits against corporations who assisted in the facilitation of human trafficking. This created another new channel for us. Savvy lawyers were using our technology and capabilities to provide case information.

Every new contract, every new client, gave us a stronger foothold and helped us extend our reach into the global war on trafficking. In 2019, we began working with the Department of Homeland Security, the state of Arizona, and other law enforcement agencies to deliver actionable intelligence for the arrest and prosecution of human traffickers. We drew the attention of the Drug Enforcement Administration, who asked us to bring a presentation to state and federal law enforcement agencies on how technology can assist with web investigations.

In the winter of 2022, we were able to help from yet another surprising angle: sports trafficking. I was invited to speak at the United Nations on the usage of technology to find individuals involved within that culture. As most Americans realize, what we call soccer (and other cultures call football) is phenomenally popular all over the world. In developing countries, traffickers use the dreams of young people to entice them, promising them a shot at being the next hero, with all the spoils that come with that success.

Sports "agents" look for aspiring athletes in South America or Africa and approach their impoverished families with breathless offers of touring the world and making loads of money through trying out for European teams. Then, after being transported to Europe or Asia, they're left high and dry, while the agents vanish with the fees they've charged. Families have usually paid far more than they could afford for these fees, often by selling their home or possessions. It's another way of creating financial profit by destroying families and using young people.

Whether I was speaking at the UN, a local church, or in a school assembly, I spoke with passion about the trafficking all around us. I often encountered audiences that were hearing of these crimes for the very first time. I sought to inspire them to get involved, and they, in turn, inspired me to keep finding new technological strategies.

Gradually, we began to see a wider awareness taking hold around us. The White House released the National Action Plan to Combat Human Trafficking in December of 2021. Among other things, it carried the understanding that with a global crisis, nations and agencies needed to cooperate. Crime syndicates needed to be identified and eliminated. At the community level, resources needed to be available for protecting the young people who are targeted by traffickers. Special hotlines were established, and in 2021, 10,360 cases of human trafficking were identified in the United States.[46]

EXPANDING THE ATTACK

Matthew Daggett of MIT Lincoln Laboratory testified before Congress in July of 2021. His entire emphasis was leveraging technology to counter the use of technology among traffickers. He described areas where gains have been made, and other areas with a deep need for development. There's plenty of tech, for example, to gather digital evidence; there's much less available to sort through it and provide what's helpful to investigators. He noted the duplication of effort in silos across the techno-landscape. We must work together.

The result has been at least one virtual workshop for large numbers of federal and state agencies, companies like ours, and other interested entities to get all of us on the same page. New tools were introduced. Everyone was interested in going after the massive, organized trafficking networks. Take down the neighborhood "recruiter," and someone will take his place quickly. The centipede has many feet; it's the head of the creature we must attack.

Sometimes, the goal is simply to disrupt the network, damage it so that it makes far less profit and is far less desirable as a criminal endeavor. Our greatest goal is to pull out these weeds by the roots.

Finding traffickers is no longer like shooting fish in a barrel, like in the days of Backpage, when they provided all their information in ads. The traffickers have come to a better understanding of the need for security. They take advantage of technology like burner phones, and they become moving targets, shifting positions too regularly for easy tracking. Those of us engaged in the hunt are using other indicators—patterns of language use in the ads, for

---

46. "National Statistics," National Human Trafficking Hotline, accessed April 23, 2024, https://humantraffickinghotline.org/en/statistics.

example. Each of us has a personal "signature" contained in how we use words. Artificial intelligence can discover and employ the clues quickly.

There are a great many other kinds of technology being developed, but the important thing is that all these approaches aid prosecutors and local investigators. In the past, it was so difficult to find and prosecute traffickers that law enforcement personnel turned to other directions—drugs or theft—where it would be easier to make an arrest and solve a case. The more we can simplify the process of locating traffickers and ensure that evidence can be compiled in these cases, the more we'll find our enforcement personnel turning their attention to this growing problem.[47]

To a rising generation of computer coders and hackers, we say, "Come one, come all." If you have tech skills, you have a choice: You can devote your life to developing video games that consume untold hours of people's time, simply for entertainment. You can pursue the next trend in social media with those skills. Or you can turn your gifts to work that saves life. Somewhere out there, I believe a gifted programmer—or two, or twenty—is reading this and realizing there's no more noble venue for the talents God has given them.

That's the realization I finally had, and now it's my life passion. How about yours?

---

47. Kylie Foy, "Turning technology against human traffickers," MIT News, May 6, 2021, https://news.mit.edu/2021/turning-technology-against-human-traffickers-0506.

15

AMAZING GRACE

Human *trafficking* is a phrase that still sounds new to many people. We think of it as an emerging crisis of our times. However, there's nothing new about it. The idea was once better known as slavery, and it's been around as long as people have. In the Bible, Joseph was trafficked by his brothers, taken to another country, and forced into labor. (See Genesis 37:26–28.)

Slavery abides, sadly, because it makes money. There was a time when slavery was so prominent and so profitable that it seemed impossible to halt. It was legal and accepted. Voices of concerned Christians—people like William Wilberforce—cried out against it, but to little avail. Wilberforce and his friends campaigned relentlessly against the ships that raided African shores and brought back young men and women forced into lifetimes of hard labor. Over time, their message began to take on momentum, and slavery was finally made illegal.

John Newton was one of the slave traders who ultimately saw the wickedness of his African voyages and taking captive helpless cargo. He'd been described as one of the most profane and rebellious men who sailed the seas. But during a fierce storm in 1748, he despaired for his life and cried out to God for rescue. He made a covenant to be a better man. From that day on, he was a devout Christian. Inevitably, his faith gave him the conviction that he couldn't live in spiritual freedom while taking other men into life-long captivity. He joined Wilberforce to crusade against the trade that had been his career.

He also wrote hymns, one of which is the most familiar Christian song in the world, "Amazing Grace." In it, he decreed that "I was blind, but now I see."

Clearly, God's hand was on John Newton, the most unlikely of prophets. Yet I believe God uplifts a new John Newton for every era. While some of us have no trouble seeing the evil in human trafficking, there are a few especially compelling voices: people who have been traffickers but have emerged to fight it.

I met my John Newton during my days as a band member on tour. Our band was in Iceland, one of my favorite stops when we toured. This trip was one of my "peak moments" because Iceland is filled with natural beauty, near endless daylight during the summer, and is the home of Sigur Rós, one of my favorite indie bands.

I was enjoying the music, breathing in the surroundings, and savoring the moment. Then I met Rodney (or at least that's the name we'll use). Rodney told me that he had once trafficked women. Then he came to know Christ, and that changed everything. After his conversion, Rodney changed his commercial sex establishment into a recovery center for people with addictions. He knew he had to be doing something that would honor God, and that's what he felt called to do. Drug addiction, he realized, is a form of slavery, too.

Almost anything in life can enslave us if we let ourselves come under its power. The only Master who will love us, heal us, and build us up is Jesus. But we live in a world full of enslavers, whether it's the lust for riches, fame, or the next high.

Rodney's passion for making a difference right where he was resonated with me. God had been working on me, too, and as much as I enjoyed music, performing for crowds, and sightseeing, I was beginning to feel a tug at my heart. Like Rodney, I needed to serve, and there were needs in this world. I well understood that, without Christ, the human heart is lost and capable of great evil. (See Jeremiah 17:9.)

As Rodney showed me what was going on in his recovery center, I understood that miracles still happen. God's redemption is more powerful than the degradation of sin. Even people capable of selling others into sexual slavery, as Rodney had done, could become front-line soldiers for Christ. John Newton's amazing grace was alive and well.

HEART TECHNOLOGY

The change in Rodney and the arc of my own life have brought me to ponder the mysteries of God's power. Perhaps the greatest theme in this trafficking book has been our belief in technology as our best tool. It's the right strategy indeed, but it's not the right power. That comes from God. All human strategies are worth little outside of what God is doing. No technology could have changed Rodney's heart. No technology could have brought me into this work. It's the technology of the human heart, as empowered by its heavenly Designer, that transforms us and the people we nurture.

I understand it this way: we are created by God to serve. We can't help but serve something or someone. For most people, it's ultimately ourselves we end up serving, and that path leads only to misery. But we can also become servants—slaves, actually—to some variation of self: personal power or fame, material gain, physical pleasure.

Then there's the road less traveled: the option of serving God. Paul (a Newton in his own day) described himself as a servant of Jesus Christ (see Romans 1:10) and said that only in such service can we attain true freedom. Only in serving Him can we master ourselves. The purveyors of human trafficking want to crush the minds and hearts of their fellow humans to profit financially. We won't catch them all, but we trust God to deal them the justice that is coming to them in time.

I need to remind myself daily that the real power comes from heaven. The same power that saved Rodney and me is the power that is still at work, recruiting soldiers to fight for His kingdom. Our finest technology is no more than the sheath we carry into battle. The sword is furnished by God. (See Ephesians 6:17.)

I pray over our lines of computer code, that they would be precise and powerful for His service.

I pray for our government and community leaders, that our tech would be able to assist them.

I pray for my limited wisdom, strength, and eloquence, that despite all my limitations I would be able to speak in schools and churches and inspire new soldiers the way past soldiers inspired me.

I pray for the broken people who are falling into this evil business, becoming modern-day enslavers and predators because they see no more decent path for their future. I pray that some loving, inspired follower of Christ will find them along the way, take mercy upon them, and help to salvage their damaged souls.

I pray for the children, the teenagers, the young people over whom this war is taking place. Our children are always our future. If they are lost, our tomorrow is lost. So I pray that God would shield them, watch over them, and protect their fragile lives.

But most of all, I pray for you, the readers, the people out there in the world, who are coming into an awareness of what we're facing; the mothers and fathers, who are comprehending the threats to their children.

I pray for those of you who know God has something special for you to do, but you haven't yet decided what it is. Consider helping us combat human trafficking. Bring your gifts, your talents, and your energy into serving God in a way that redeems lives.

We call it dark traffic, and sometimes the darkness seems impenetrable. But we know that light is undefeated against darkness, and the light of God is infinite.

All we need to do is shed the light that God gives us. Will you come and shine the light with us?

ABOUT THE AUTHORS

NOEL THOMAS

Noel Thomas, a passionate abolitionist in the fight against human trafficking, brings a unique blend of experience and expertise to the forefront of his work. As the former statewide anti-trafficking coordinator for the State of Florida, Thomas has dedicated his career to combatting one of the most pressing issues of our time.

Thomas's journey began as a passionate advocate, working tirelessly to raise awareness about human trafficking and implement effective strategies for prevention and intervention. His invaluable contributions as the statewide anti-trafficking coordinator earned him recognition for his commitment and results.

Building on his success in Florida, Thomas took on the role of CEO at Dark Watch, an organization committed to shedding light on the shadows of human trafficking. Under his leadership, Dark Watch has become a beacon of hope, providing technology to the frontlines of counter trafficking. .Thomas has taken his advocacy to the global stage, as a guest panelist at the United Nations. His insights and expertise have been instrumental in shaping policies and strategies to combat human trafficking. Thomas's contributions to these critical discussions reflect not only his deep understanding of the issue but also his unwavering commitment to creating a world free from the chains of modern-day slavery.

ROB SUGGS

A versatile and creative author, editor, and storyteller, Rob Suggs has written or collaborated on more than sixty books.

His clients have included *New York Times* best-selling authors such as Kyle Idleman, Lee Strobel, Mark Batterson, David Jeremiah, and Bruce Wilkinson. He worked with Jeremy and Jennifer Williams on *Tenacious: How God Used a Terminal Diagnosis to Turn a Family and a Football Team into Champions*, which is being turned into a movie.

Rob co-authored several books with family counselor Dr. Ross Campbell, including *How to Really Love Your Angry Child*. Among Rob's solo efforts are *The Comic Book Bible, Christmas Ate My Family*, and *Top Dawg: Mark Richt and the Revival of Georgia Football*.

A graduate of Furman University, Rob served for three years as a senior editor at Walk Through the Bible Ministries. An experienced teacher and preacher, Rob has led a four-part seminar on how the Bible came to be. He wrote and illustrated a six-part history of Christianity for *His* magazine published by InterVarsity Press. He wrote the LifeGuide Bible studies *The Ten Commandments* and *Christian Community*, and *The Book that Conquered Time*.

For two decades, Rob contributed many cartoons to *Christianity Today* and *Leadership Journal*. Collections of these cartoons were published in the books *It Came from Beneath the Pew* and *Preacher from the Black Lagoon*.

Rob is a fourth-generation native of Atlanta, Georgia. He and his wife Gayle have two adult children. Readers may connect with Rob at www.robsuggs.com.